The Bottom Line for Children's Programs

What You Need to Know to Manage the Money

D1593990

The Bottom Line
for Children's Programs

What You Need to Know to Manage the Money

Gwen G. Morgan
Wheelock College

Steam Press  Watertown, Massachusetts
Distributed by Gryphon House, Inc.

Copyright 1982, 1984, and 1989 by Gwen G. Morgan, titled
"Managing the Day Care Dollars." Current (1999), expanded
and re-titled, "The Bottom Line for Children's Programs."

ISBN: 0-942820-49-5
Library of Congress Catalog Card Number: 82-050691

Distributed by Gryphon House, Inc.
P.O. Box 207
Beltsville, MD 20704-0207 USA

Additional copies of this book are available through
bookstores, or directly from Gryphon House.

Manufactured in the United States of America

Table of Contents

Preface

This financial handbook is intended as a guide and reference to the concepts necessary for good financial management of children's programs. By children's programs, I refer to part-day and full-day early care and education programs, Head Start, Early Intervention programs, programs for out-of-school time, schools, and other education and human service agencies. The examples I use are drawn primarily from full-day child care centers, because: (1) child care agencies are often single-center organizations, responsible for both sides of the budget; (2) child care budget materials are simple in contrast to those of larger organizations, and (3) they are probably as challenging as financial materials can be, since they balance so close to the break-even point.

Financial management is focused on the future, and is not the same as accounting. The book is useful for anyone who now has, or may in the future have, responsibility for an educational organization or one that delivers human services. Such a person may be called director, administrator, manager, executive, leader, or other title; I use these terms interchangeably. Administrators in some systems may not be fully responsible for the income side of the budget, but the tools described will enable them to move laterally and vertically to other settings in their careers that need the broader scope of skills.

Since its original publication in 1982, this book has been revised a number of times. This 1999 edition, a thorough revision of the entire text, updates the legal and financial information, adds new explanations, and presents new material, including a substantial section of case examples that can be used by groups of directors for self-study, or by college instructors of administration classes.

The handbook has grown out of sharing among administrators of school-age and early childhood programs from all sections of the country who have participated in the Advanced Management Seminars in Early Care and Education at Wheelock College since 1975. This book is indebted most of all to administrators: to those many participants who worked hard together to develop these ideas and apply them to children's program management. I would particularly like to acknowledge four early participants: Nancy Travis, Roger Neugebauer, Carl Staley, and Joe Perrault, all pioneer leaders and sharers in the development of management resources. Recently, Carl Staley has been of enormous help in updating the materials for this edition. In addition, some of the mini-case assignments were developed by Cliff Baden and Andi Genser, who taught a graduate course in financial management at Wheelock.

Finally, I would like to thank Wheelock College itself, its Presidents since 1974, its Graduate School, and its Deans, for their continuing support in the development of coursework geared to meet the needs of children's program administrators. Their support began at a time when there were almost no other educational programs of this nature.

Gwen G. Morgan

Budget is Policy

If you are responsible for managing a children's program, you must be able to understand, plan and control its finances. This work typically requires a new set of central and critical skills.

Many directors of human services and educational programs come to their positions through working directly with children and their families. Without training or experience in financial management, they may believe they can turn the financial aspect of the program over to somebody else, while retaining control of the program's policy decisions. Such a belief is totally wrong. No director can influence policy without influencing the budget process and decisions. **Budget is policy.**

The budget is the intentional allocation of a program's resources, without which policy cannot be implemented. By generating reports that bring information to decisionmakers when they need it, a director can use the budget to guide policy throughout the year.

All we dream and aspire to accomplish for children, families, and the community is expressed in the budget in the language of money. Every line item in the budget states a policy decision that directly determines the nature and quality of the program. Whoever makes the budget is making these policy decisions.

Who Makes the Budget?

In a proprietary (owner-operated) organization, the owner-operator and any director employed to manage the program should prepare an annual budget. In a small corporation, the director, sometimes with the treasurer, prepares an annual budget, which is then fully discussed and formally approved by the board. In a not-for-profit corporation, the treasurer prepares a year-end report to explain to the board just how successful last year's budget was.

When a children's program is part of a larger program (as in a campus child care center, many Head Start programs, or a corporate chain), the budget may be created at the level of the larger organization. However, monitoring expenditures will be the responsibility of the administrator, who will need to generate financial reports for running the center, as well as reports to the larger organization. Such administrators sometimes need to re-create their own budgets for management purposes.

The director, and not the accountant, is responsible for developing the budget. Accountants are invaluable to children's programs as financial historians. They can track down what money came in and how it was spent, with precision. They can tell you exactly where you stand if you should have to close down your children's program, and they can tell you what you are worth if you need to borrow money. This kind of information is absolutely essential. You will need an accountant or accountant services, but not for developing the budget.

As the person who prepares the annual budget, the administrator is responsible for making informed decisions about the future. Internally and externally, the budget serves as an important policy statement. It tells responsible planners within the organization and its funding sources, and also the outside world, what the program intends to do in the coming year and how it will be able to do it.

The Budget Process

A budget projection, or a pro forma budget, means a best guess about what the income and expenses will be for the year to come, based when possible on the experience of the year just ended. Budgets should always be marked with the period of time they cover.

The budget is most useful when it is treated as an official document from which one would not lightly depart. If, for any reason, things do not work out as intended, of course you will have to change your plans. If anticipated income does not materialize, or if necessary expenditures are larger than expected, the center cannot stick to a spending plan for money it does not have.

Most experts recommend keeping the original approved annual budget even in the face of changed conditions, and simply voting or adopting amendments with explanatory notes to be attached to the budget, making it clear why the changes are being made. Even an owner-operator in full control of the budget should make and respect an annual budget, making and documenting dated changes, in preference to making frequent new budgets.

Two Sides to a Budget

A budget always has two sides, two different aspects of the year's plan. There is the *income* (or *revenues*) side, which documents expected income by sources; and the *expenditure* side, which itemizes all the expected expense for the year. The two sides must balance, i.e., there must be at least as much income as expenses. It should be obvious that if one side changes, the other side must change accordingly. If the budget is out of balance, the options are quite limited. Either the spending plan will have to change at once, so that the program is not spending money it does not have, or a feasible new plan must be made to increase income at once.

Starting with Two Different Kinds of Budget Projection

Make your operating budget first. New programs, or programs adding a service or making a significant expansion, will need to make two budgets: a *start-up budget* and an *annual operating budget.* Because start-up problems come first, they tend to loom large. But it is a very serious mistake to embark on start-up expenses without a very firm plan for where the operating money is going to come from. Start-up costs are difficult to muster, but they are insignificant when compared with the day-in and day-out costs of operating a program over the long haul. Avoid the mistake of incurring start-up expenses without having planned for sources of operating money.

Start-up costs include all the one-time-only costs of getting started, including the costs of getting a building ready to house a children's program; the costs of planning; and the costs of recruiting and training the new staff. For a start-up period, you expect and plan for the cost of a period of under-utilization, during which time the program has not yet enrolled the full number of children it will eventually serve. During this period, the program is not operating efficiently; that is to say, it is not operating at or above the break-even point. This start-up period will have to draw on some working capital to cover costs incurred before the first income is received.

Start-up costs, unless tiny, should not be included in the first year's operating budget, as they will inflate the expenditure side of the budget (and thus the cost for each child) beyond a feasible limit. It will then be impossible to figure how to price the service offered.

The annual operating budget is a list of all the items on which money will have to be spent once the program is under way and operating at close to its full-planned capacity. At this point, with all the planned income coming in, and all the planned expenses going out, the center is financially stable. That is why it is important to make the annual operating budget first. If you can show, in numbers, that the budget can balance once it has started up, then it is feasible to start. This annual budget is a feasibility exercise for a new program.

Making an annual operating budget enables you to estimate a per-child cost. An operating budget for a year and a start-up budget are presented in the next section. For directors, board members, or planners who have never constructed a budget, these budgets can be used as exercises for developing the necessary budget skills.

Some Crude Rules of Thumb for Planning

There is no such thing as "the cost" of an early childhood program in absolute terms. Your costs are determined by what you must spend, what you want to spend, and what you have available to spend. You *must* spend as required by law in the licensing requirements, federal and state labor policies, specifications of any source of subsidy. You *want* to spend according to your own vision of excellence for your center, and your own goals. What you *have available* to spend brings reality into your planning.

Before you make the budget, it may be helpful to think about your costs and their feasibility through some crude planning formulas. Richard Ruopp developed a quick way of guessing at the order of magnitude of a child care center's costs:

- First, ask yourself what you think a classroom teacher should be paid, on average.
- Second, ask yourself for how many children a classroom teacher should be responsible (the ratio of children to staff).
- Third, divide the amount a classroom teacher should be paid by the number of children per staff.
- Fourth, multiply that number by two, since classroom staff constitute about half the total budget of a child care center, with administration, supplies, equipment, and the facility responsible for the other half.

The formula is:

(Salary of one teacher/year ÷ the # of children per staff member) × 2 = cost/child/year.

That is, a center that pays its teachers, on average, $16,000 per year to be responsible for eight children needs at least an income of roughly $4,000 per child per year. **Unless the center has some other source of income enabling it to exclude some of its costs in the fees it charges, it must charge enough to cover all its expenditures.**

Parents earning the median income probably cannot afford to pay more than 10% of their total family income for fees for all their children's programs. (See median income chart on the following page.) Parents at upper income levels can probably pay more, but might not be willing. Parents at half the median cannot pay as much as 10% of their income for fees for all their children, because most of their income goes for shelter, taxes and food. Poor parents have trouble making ends meet to cover the necessities of life.

The *median* is the middle figure in a list of figures arranged from lowest to highest. It is a way of identifying what most families earn, rather than an average amount that everybody earns. A table of median incomes for a family of four is available each year from the government. The national median is now around $45,000. Of course planners will be most interested in the expected incomes of the families that live near the program they hope to operate, rather than statewide or national medians.

FAMILY MEDIAN INCOMES 1998

State	Income	State	Income
Alabama	$38,700	Montana	$37,500
Alaska	53,900	Nebraska	45,700
Arizona	43,500	Nevada	49,800
Arkansas	34,700	New Hampshire	49,800
California	52,600	New Jersey	61,200
Colorado	49,300	New Mexico	38,000
Connecticut	60,400	New York	50,700
Delaware	53,700	North Carolina	42,200
D.C.	51,100	North Dakota	39,300
Florida	42,400	Ohio	46,400
Georgia	44,200	Oklahoma	36,500
Hawaii	56,500	Oregon	43,200
Idaho	41,300	Pennsylvania	43,400
Illinois	53,200	Rhode Island	47,100
Indiana	46,100	South Carolina	40,600
Iowa	44,500	South Dakota	39,500
Kansas	45,500	Tennessee	41,000
Kentucky	36,400	Texas	42,900
Louisiana	35,200	Utah	45,200
Maine	37,800	Vermont	40,700
Maryland	59,200	Virginia	49,900
Massachusetts	54,200	Washington	49,000
Michigan	49,800	West Virginia	32,300
Minnesota	51,800	Wisconsin	48,200
Mississippi	33,000	Wyoming	42,000
Missouri	44,300	U.S.	45,300

A final, crude rule of thumb for planning is comparing the proportion of the expenditures for different parts of a budget. For child care, an early study examined the relative percentage of the child care budget for different functions. *(A Study in Child Care, 1970-71, Cambridge, MA: Abt Associates, April 1971 Table IV, p. 20.)*

This first cost analysis study in 20 exemplary child care centers was done in 1970. Although the level of expenditure is different today, the method of analyzing costs remains the same, and the percentages spent on different functions is not greatly different from those of the first study. In 1970, the following percentages were being spent in standardized cost categories. (How to do a functional cost analysis will be explained later in this book.)

FUNCTIONAL COSTS, IN PERCENTAGES

Child care and teaching	70% to 37% range	.... 50% average
Administration	27% to 8% range	.... 16% average
Feeding	19% to 6% range	.... 11% average
Health	14% to 0% range	..... 4% average
Occupancy	22% to 9% range	.... 13% average
Other (transportation, social services, etc.)	23% to 0% range	..... 6% average
TOTAL EXPENSES		**100%**

Although these costs vary greatly, depending on the availability of low cost or free space or services, they do give some guidance. For example, if the annual costs of a building and utilities under consideration were 25% of total planned expenditures for the function "Occupancy," it is likely that the program might not be able to survive, since that percentage is above the top of the range of costs.

Functional cost analysis continues to be an important tool in comparing early care and education expenditures. A recent study *(The Cost, Quality, and Child Outcomes Study, S. Helburn and Study Team, 1995, University of Colorado, Denver CO.)* found that, in general, for-profit centers pay a higher percentage of their total expenditures for occupancy, while non-profits pay a higher percentage of their total expenditures for staff salaries. These data reflect the fact that for-profit centers are less frequently able to operate in donated space.

Public school budgets are not comparable to those of private organizations, unless some standardizing format, such as functional analysis, is used to make them comparable. In general, you can assume that public school budgets do not include any costs of their physical space, and that they do include salaries, but not benefits.

Making the Budget

Not all directors are responsible for all aspects of the budget, as explained above. As part of a larger organization, you may be expected to have limited budget participation, such as only controlling expenditures. You will find, however, that your ability to achieve quality is limited when your budget participation is limited. Many directors in large organizations have found it important to reconstruct their own budget for their own management purposes. That way, they have a check to make sure they are getting timely information from the larger organization, and have the knowledge to raise issues and to participate in discussions about the budget.

This book assumes that budget skills and knowledge are important to any director. If your budget role is limited, that situation could change if the organization changes in the direction of more site-based management. Full budget skills may be required of you in your next position. On the following page you will find a budget checklist, followed by a *line-item budget.* A line-item budget consists of a list of items, one item per line, and a corresponding dollar figure to represent expenditure for the item or income from the item.

Before you make your budget, you will need to gather the information on the checklist, which will require some decision-making and a day or two for research. The budget notes that follow give some ideas for figuring the costs. You will need to create your own budget notes to help you remember and explain how you decided on the numbers you used for each line item.

You will notice that the budget that follows uses a "utilization factor" to adjust expected income. Utilization is further explained in Section 3 of this handbook: **The Income Side of the Budget.**

Expenditures: A Budget Checklist

A. Employees

___ 1. Budget salaries for all personnel positions, whether full-time or part-time. Remember to include office staff, maintenance workers, snow plow, cook, and anybody else who will be on your payroll.

___ 2. Budget for raises, if you expect to raise pay.

___ 3. Budget substitute-time for the time regular staff will not be in the class-room, including: sick leave, family and medical leave, vacations, compensatory time, and work release time for training.

___ 4. Budget for the employer's share of Social Security tax, which is required by law. In 1999, the employer's share is 7.65%. Do not budget the employee's contribution, since it is already included in the salary.

___ 5. Budget for Worker's Compensation Insurance. Each state has different rules, and some small, new programs may not be required to have coverage.

___ 6. Budget for Unemployment Insurance. This is not a major expense. Your program will be experience-rated after you have been in operation and should receive a rate notification annually. The agency that administers unemployment in your state can explain this rating to you.

___ 7. Decide on and budget for the benefits you will offer full-time and part-time staff on your payroll, in addition to the benefits that you must, by law, provide, including: health insurance, retirement plan, child care.

___ 8. If you provide child care as a benefit, remember to include its cost to your program as a budget expense.

B. Consultant and Contract Services

___ 1. Decide what consultants you will pay, if any. Examples: doctor, dentist, psychologist, nutritionist, training specialist, outside speakers.

___ 2. Decide what services you will use in place of employed staff. Examples: cleaning services, accounting services, payroll services, food services.

___ 3. Include the cost of subscriptions, books, and memberships in professional organizations.

C. Occupancy

___ 1. Include rent or mortgage payment. Check to see if any changes are planned for next year. If so, be sure to include the increase in your projections.

___ 2. Budget for maintenance of building and grounds, including a regular schedule for repair and upkeep. Include snow plowing. Use prior records if available, and allow for rising costs.

___ 3. Check on possible rate increases as you budget for fuel, light, telephone and water.

D. Supplies and Equipment

___ 1. Include here all materials that you will use up during the year.

___ 2. Itemize supplies by category: office, classroom, and playground supplies; food and kitchen supplies; laundry and housekeeping supplies; health supplies, etc.

___ 3. Don't include all the equipment you have bought as start-up, if you are a new program. Do budget in the operating budget for a planned five-year schedule of replacement, or, if you are for-profit, follow the Internal Revenue Service's rules for depreciation.

E. Conferences and Training

___ 1. Remember to budget sending staff to regional and national conferences each year.

___ 2. If you are going to give release time to staff so they can take courses, remember to budget for substitutes.

F. Other

___ 1. When figuring transportation costs, include vehicles, gas, oil, tires, mileage and repairs.

___ 2. Check with your insurance representative about possible rate changes.

___ 3. Remember to include costs of license, building approvals, and related costs. Include them in your start-up budget the first year. After that, they become operating costs.

___ 4. Include in your operating costs any interest payments you will have to make for loans and/or other sources of borrowed revenues. The principal will not be in your budget, but you will show it on a balance sheet. [See Balance Sheets.]

___ 5. Include a small, miscellaneous account to cover unanticipated costs that do not fit other categories.

*Note that Petty Cash is not a budget item. Petty cash is a **way** of spending money, and can fall into any budget category.*

Form for a Simple, Line-Item Budget for Annual Center Operation

Face Sheet: Annual Budget for Fiscal Year _____

INCOME

Fees from parents	$	_____
Fees from state/local government		_____
Other government sources		_____
Registration fees		_____
Special fees and sales		_____
Transportation charges		_____
USDA Food Program		_____
Gifts, contributions, unrestricted use		_____
Gifts, contributions restricted to special uses		_____
Investment income		_____
Sale or exchange of property		_____
Miscellaneous		_____
TOTAL INCOME	$	_____
Income adjusted by utilization factor	$	_____

EXPENDITURES

Personnel	$	_____
Fringes @ _____%		_____
Special fees, contract services & consultants		_____
Supplies		_____
Occupancy		_____
Interest on loans		_____
Furniture, vehicles and equipment		_____
Conferences, workshops, special events		_____
Other expenses		_____
TOTAL EXPENSES	$	_____
Number of children full-time		_____
Number of FTE children (Full-time spaces shared by attending part-time children)		_____
Total number of expected FT and FTE		_____
TOTAL PER-CHILD COST	$	_____

Form for a Budget Back-Up Sheet with Detail for the Line-Item Budget

1. PERSONNEL EXPENDITURES

(Use extra pages as needed)

TITLE	NAME	SALARY/MO. OR SALARY/YR.	% TIME EMPLOYED	ANNUAL PAY

List administrative/clerical staff

_____ _____ _____ _____ _____
_____ _____ _____ _____ _____
_____ _____ _____ _____ _____
_____ _____ _____ _____ _____

List classroom staff

_____ _____ _____ _____ _____
_____ _____ _____ _____ _____
_____ _____ _____ _____ _____
_____ _____ _____ _____ _____
_____ _____ _____ _____ _____
_____ _____ _____ _____ _____
_____ _____ _____ _____ _____
_____ _____ _____ _____ _____

List social service/parent coordinator staff

_____ _____ _____ _____ _____

List maintenance staff

_____ _____ _____ _____ _____

Cook

_____ _____ _____ _____ _____

List health staff, any other staff

_____ _____ _____ _____ _____

SUB-TOTAL PAYROLL _____

2. FRINGE BENEFITS

Employer share of Social Security tax (FICA) _____
Worker's Compensation _____
Health insurance _____
Child care benefit _____
Other benefits _____

SUB-TOTAL FRINGE BENEFITS _____

Form continues on the next page

3. PROFESSIONAL FEES, CONTRACT SERVICES AND CONSULTANTS

Maintenance contract _____

Catered food _____

Transportation, portal to portal contract _____

Health services, contracted or consultant _____

Training, contracted or consultant _____

Legal services _____

Payroll services _____

Accounting services _____

Other _____

SUBTOTAL PROFESSIONAL FEES AND CONTRACTS _____

Value of donated professional services (_____)

4. SUPPLIES

Teaching/care giving supplies _____

Food supplies, kitchen supplies _____

Office supplies _____

Building, grounds and maintenance supplies _____

Health supplies _____

Housekeeping supplies _____

Vehicle supplies _____

Health supplies _____

Other consumable supplies _____

SUB-TOTAL SUPPLIES _____

Value of donated supplies (_____)

5. OCCUPANCY

Rent _____

Real estate taxes _____

Maintenance and repairs _____

Amortization on leasehold improvement _____

Utilities _____

Building insurance _____

Interest on mortgage (if building owned) _____

Depreciation (building only) _____

Other building occupancy costs _____

SUB-TOTAL OCCUPANCY COSTS _____

Dollar value of donated space or land (_____)

6. FURNITURE, EQUIPMENT AND VEHICLES

Office furniture and equipment _____

Building equipment _____

Teaching/child care furniture & equipment _____

Kitchen equipment _____

Vehicle equipment   _____
Other   _____
Total purchase cost, rental, or installment payment of
   furniture, equipment, and vehicles   _____
Depreciation on furniture, equipment, and vehicles   _____
Maintenance and repairs:
   Office furniture and equipment   _____
   Building equipment   _____
   Teaching and child care furniture & equipment   _____
   Kitchen equipment   _____
   Other   _____
Total maintenance and repairs   _____
Other   _____
          SUB-TOTAL FURNITURE, EQUIPMENT AND VEHICLES   _____
   Dollar value of donated furniture, equipment and vehicles   (_____)

7. CONFERENCES, WORKSHOPS AND EVENTS

Expenses (food, transportation, child care etc.) for board meetings,
   advisory groups, community relations, fund raising   _____
Expenses, conferences and workshops for staff   _____
Fees or transportation for family services outside center   _____
Expenses (food, transportation, child care, etc.) for parent
   social activities, parent education, parent conferences   _____
Special events, services, field trips   _____
Other   _____
          SUB-TOTAL SPECIAL EVENTS   _____
   Dollar value of donated goods and services   (_____)

8. OTHER EXPENSES

Advertising, printing and outside duplicating   _____
Telephone, fax, e-mail   _____
Postage, mailing, express delivery   _____
Professional memberships   _____
Bank charges, interest   _____
Licenses and permits; transportation insurance   _____
Uncollectible accounts (bad debts)   _____
Contingency fund; payment to reserve   _____
Loss from fire, theft, or vandalism   _____
Indirect administrative expense of sponsoring organization,
   franchise, or corporate expense where applicable   _____
Other   _____
          SUB-TOTAL OTHER EXPENSES   _____
   Dollar value of in-kind donations (describe)   (_____)
          GRAND TOTAL ALL EXPENSES   _____
          GRAND TOTAL DONATED VALUE   (_____)

Budget Justification

A *budget justification* (or *rationale*) is a line-by-line narrative, summarizing the reasoning that led you to arrive at the figures you are using. These notes are important to help anyone else understand your calculations and you will find them essential yourself when you are trying to remember the basis for your figures months after you made the budget. At the very least, you will keep on file notes that explain all your calculations. The following notes will give you some of the information that you might include in your budget notes. I strongly urge you to prepare a budget justification.

1. Personnel

List your staff by title, and by name if they are already employed, as follows:

> Executive Director, Jane Jones, @ $3000/mo. (100% time), $36,000/yr.
>
> Cook, Julietta Cabrese, 4 hrs./day @ $5.50 hr., $5,500/yr.
>
> Floater, Ramona Bird, @ $12,480/yr.

If you pay employees to plow snow, do maintenance and repairs, etc., budget their salaries under Personnel.

If you are starting a new program, you may not know exactly what each employee is going to earn, and you will budget a salary *range*, with the actual salary depending on each staff member's level of education and longevity, such as:

> Executive Director: . . . . $ 26,000 - $37,000/yr.
>
> Assistant Director: . . . . $ 22,000 - $26,000/yr.
>
> Lead Teacher: . . . . $ 17,000 - $22,000/yr.
>
> Teacher: . . . . $ 15,000 - $18,000/yr.
>
> Assistant Teacher: . . . . $ 12,000 - $ 15,000/yr.

If you run an existing program, you will know the salaries staff currently earn, and you will budget for salary increases according to some predictable schedule. See a sample salary schedule on page 33. Note that in the sample scale, Fairchild rewards two factors: longevity of employment at Fairchild, and increased training and qualifications. Its salary policy therefore offers incentives for the characteristics it wants to encourage in its staff: decreased turnover and increased competency.

Budget substitute time for all positions that require substitutes, and explain the basis for your estimates. Substitutes are needed when your regular staff members are sick, on leave or on vacation; have compensatory time off; or have released-time for training. You might also need substitutes if a staff member should have to leave suddenly.

2. Fringe Benefits

There are two kinds of fringe benefits: *voluntary* and *mandatory.* The voluntary benefits are those voluntarily offered by the organization, and included in its contract with the employees. The mandatory benefits are those required by law. Check carefully on all fringe benefits every year, since laws and insurance rates may change.

Once you know the salaries and fringes, you will be able to calculate what you offer in benefits, both voluntary and mandatory, as a percentage of the total salaries of those receiving the benefits. It will probably be between 15% and 30% of salaries. Be sure to apply this quick computation only to the salaries of those employees who receive all the benefits. You might have to figure part-time employees at a different rate if you do not offer them the voluntary benefits that full-time employees receive. All employees must receive all mandatory benefits.

Voluntary, or non-mandatory benefits, include the center's expense for:

(a) Employees' *life insurance* or *retirement plan,* if any. Many children's programs do not offer these benefits. Rather than not offering an insurance plan, programs that cannot afford to share in the cost of such a benefit have sometimes been able to make the benefits available to employees who wish to pay the full cost at a group rate. Budget only the employer's contribution, not the employees' contributions.

(b) Employees' *health benefits,* if any. More children's programs now pay health benefits than in the past, but there are still many employees not yet covered. Justify your health benefits in budget notes using this format as an example:

Health insurance @ $300/mo. x 8 employees x 12 months = $28,800

(c) Employees' *child care benefits,* if any. If your center offers free or reduced-price child care, budget its total cost to the center.

Mandatory benefits include:

(a) The Federal Insurance Contributions Act (FICA) is a payroll tax to pay for *social security benefits.* As of 1999, the employer share of this tax is 7.65% of each salary. An entry in the budget justification might look like this:

FICA @ 7.65% x $75,000 = $5,738

The employee is also required to contribute the same amount to FICA, but you will not budget the employee's contribution, which, conceptually, you pay the employee as salary. (See **Withholding,** on the next page.)

(b) *Worker's Compensation Plan* is an insurance plan (into which the employer is required by law to pay) that covers the company against the cost of employee claims for unemployment compensation. Laws differ in the 50 states regarding the size of organizations covered by Worker's Compensation, and the percentage of money paid to the state versus the percentage paid to the federal government. Check with your insurance agent or your accountant to get your state's most recent provisions.

Even if not required to participate, employers may choose to cover potential future claims, which they will have to pay themselves if not covered by unemployment insurance.

Withholding taxes that the employee will owe the government is not a benefit. Withholding the employees' share of FICA, or state or federal income tax is the employer's obligation to the government. For budget purposes, that amount remains in the employee's salary. Be sure to withhold the correct amount from every paycheck and place it in a special bank account before paying it to the government. When you pay your employees, you should let them know how much of their salary is being withheld for FICA and for the employee's income tax. You pay this money to the government four times a year. **It is a crime for you to spend any of the withheld money at any time. This money is not a part of your operating funds.**

Every employee signs a withholding tax form W-4, to specify how much money should be taken out of the salary to pay federal income tax. If the employees are eligible for any tax credits or deductions, this form will guide you on what amount to withhold from their salary so that only the taxes they will owe are withheld.

3. Professional Fees and Contract Services

In this final section of your personnel expenditures, you include all services provided by people who are not on your regular payroll; consultants and services you are securing by contract or on a retainer basis. This category would include: fees for speech and physical therapists and curriculum specialists, if you pay such fees; payments made to doctors, nurses, dentists, hospitals and clinics, if you make such payments; and all fees for professional consultation in administration, accounting services, training, legal services and the like. Transportation for field trips would not be included here.

No fringe benefits are paid for contract services and consultants. As independent contractors, or consultants, these individuals pay for their own benefits. The criteria for determining that a person is an independent contractor and not an employee are:

- the employer sets the hours for employees, but not for independent contractors;
- the employer defines the job for employees, but not for independent contractors;
- the employer does not control how the independent contractor does the job, but does control how the employee does the job;
- the independent contractor determines the price paid for the work; the employer sets salaries for employees.

4. Supplies

This part of the budget covers all materials that will be totally consumed (used up) within the budget year, or will not last longer than a year, and all equipment that costs less than $250. Note that the budget back-up sheet separates different kinds of supplies; i.e., classroom supplies, office supplies, food supplies, maintenance supplies, vehicle supplies, health supplies. You need not make these distinctions in your line-item budget, but keeping track of them separately will help you later, when you are trying to understand your costs.

5. Occupancy

This section explains all the costs arising from a program's building and land use, including all donations of space and land. If a center pays rent that does not include all utility costs, it may have certain additional line items that describe these costs. If a center owns a building, it may have mortgage payments and real estate taxes.

Maintenance and repairs covers all payments to outside vendors, but not to center staff, for: repair; maintenance; gardening; rubbish removal; window washing; painting; plumbing; carpentry; dry cleaning of drapes, rugs, and furniture; repair or maintenance of furnace, boilers, kitchen, bathroom, and playground equipment; and minor building improvements. Snow removal can be listed as a separate line item, or can be included in this category.

Utilities covers payments of electricity, gas, oil, and water, but not the telephone, copier, or computer equipment, which would be listed separately or under office equipment.

Building insurance covers all insurance associated with occupancy, including fire, theft, windstorm, and public liability insurance.

Depreciation is the cost of a building maintenance or repair in excess of $250, all of which may be depreciated to reflect the decline in value over time.

Amortization of leasehold building improvements is a way of spreading the center's building improvement costs (more than $250) over a period of several years in the center's budget.

Donated space means the fair market value or rental value of donated property or the excess of such fair value over the rent actually paid. (See additional section on **In-Kind and Donations,** on the next page.)

6. Furniture, Equipment, and Vehicles

This budget section refers to equipment that will not be used up in a year, in contrast to the supplies covered in category 4, above. In this category, you will budget replacement costs on equipment that may wear out during the year, as opposed to the initial new equipment you included in the start-up budget, or amortized beyond the first year. This item covers the costs necessary to replace such equipment on a regular schedule.

Depreciation may be budgeted over the useful life of an item, using IRS guidelines. The Federal Internal Revenue Service has established expected, useful lives for large items of equipment. Its regulations determine how to compute what these items would be worth after 1 year, after 2 years, and so on down to the point where each is worth nothing. For-profit organizations should figure the depreciation on their equipment, and should check IRS guidelines for any changes. Do not use replacement cost, or new equipment cost, for fair market value.

Depreciation is less useful as a tool for tax-exempt organizations, which generally replace equipment on a rotating schedule, spending the same amount each year to replace different equipment.

7. Special Events and Services

This section includes various meetings and event expenses, exclusive of staff costs already budgeted in the personnel sections. Expenses for parent development, staff development, board development, field trips, and other meetings and events are budgeted here.

8. Other Expenses

When budgeting for *telephones,* remember to include installation costs. Check with the telephone company, your insurance agent, and others about possible increases. Should you incur loss from fire, theft, or vandalism, whether or not there is insurance to cover the loss, enter it as an expense. Any insurance payments you receive will be reported as income. Shop for the best *liability insurance coverage* and rates, since variations may be great. If not budgeted elsewhere, include cost of *computer service fees, Internet fees, modem charges, and photocopier service fees.* If you use a consultant or consultant services to help with computer use, budget these costs under consultant and contracted services.

Indirect costs must also be considered. Some programs that are sub-parts of a larger organization, such as a college, a multi-service agency, or a large corporation, will also budget a cost figure to cover the sponsoring organization's overhead costs, such as bookkeeping, fund raising, payroll, oversight, maintenance, utility costs, and the like. These items, if known, can be budgeted as separate line items, but some costs will be estimates, such as percentage of the chief administrator's time.

If the program is federally funded, the government may conduct an audit to establish an indirect cost figure. This cost figure will then be fixed for the program as a percentage, governing future federally funded projects. The program can use this established indirect cost percentage as a rationale for overhead in other budgets.

Also to be included in the "indirect expense" category are payments made to franchise holding companies by franchisees, and any expense to the larger corporation incurred as part of a service contract by a national corporation.

Additional Information about In-Kind and Donated Goods and Services

The budget guides on the preceding pages include space for figuring the value of donated aspects of the children's program, even though these do not represent actual cash expenditures of cash income. **These aspects of a program's budget will not necessarily affect its pricing, and are therefore included in parentheses whenever listed.**

The concept of "in-kind" has been used in two different ways. One was developed by the American Institute of Certified Public Accountants (AICPA) to help programs to recognize in their financial reports anything that was being given to a program that would have had to be purchased if it were not being given. Without recognizing the value of this component in financial reports, the organization would not get a true picture of its costs and its financial situation. One center with a strong donated component could not be financially compared with one that had to pay cash for this component.

A classic example would be a child care program operated by a church with a budget that shows no cost for rent or utilities. Comparing that program's "cost of care" with that of the program across the street that has to pay rent does not reveal the true financial situation. Children's programs operated by schools, universities, Head Start, hospitals and other large organizations have often had part of their true operating cost paid for out of other budgets.

In-kind has developed another meaning in the Head Start system. Head Start programs have been under pressure to generate in-kind matching local contributions as required by the Head Start legislation. Head Start's regulations have allowed the recognition of some in-kind contributions that would not have been purchased if they had had been given, thereby failing to meet the standards of AICPA.

Therefore, your budget notes should make clear what standards you are using for listing in-kind contributions. There are many reasons why you, your funding source, the parents, and the general public should have access to knowledge of the full value of your program. For one thing, it is not possible to compare costs from one program to another without some standard approach to costs, as well as information about what resources, in addition to money, a program is using. Further, the general public and the policymakers lack a sense of the valuable assets that are represented by all these children's programs and their more than 100-year history of assets and resources.

When determining the cash costs of a program, do not include the donated or in-kind items. They should be added to the cash costs only when determining the true value of the program.

An in-kind donation is defined as any goods or services *donated* to your children's program. It means anything of value that is used by the program in providing its service, that was not purchased out of the budget; or any services performed by a person not on the payroll and not paid as a consultant or independent contractor.

Examples of In-Kind Services

Ideally, you will know what the in-kind items of your budget are, so that you can demonstrate the value of the service you are providing and the true costs of providing it. In-kind can include:

- Food donated by a parent, volunteer, or friend for a party, picnic, or special occasion
- Art supplies, toys, equipment donated by friends or community groups
- Toys to be given to the children at holidays or birthdays
- Clothing given to be distributed to the children
- Visits by the librarian, on her day off, for story hour
- Vision, teeth, sickle cell, and other screening
- Regular volunteers (who should sign-in)
- Professional services at which a person is expert, rendered by a parent or a friend, such as emergency plumbing, electrical repairs, heating, etc.
- Services rendered to the center's program by a parent or a friend: repairing toys or books, sewing curtains, making equipment, rebinding blankets, painting, organizing play areas, etc.
- Office-related services rendered by a parent or a friend: typing, bookkeeping, telephoning, carpooling, etc.
- Activity-related services rendered by parents, friends, and volunteers: storytelling, assisting with field trips, etc.
- Visits by groups to entertain children: puppet theatre, Girl Scouts, Boy Scouts, singing groups, etc.
- Visits by children to the fire house, barber shop, museum, etc., if someone at these places takes time to explain his occupation or act as a guide to the children, and/or if there is usually an admission fee that has been waived

Criteria for a Donation

A donation, to be included, should meet the following criteria:

- It should have a measurable market value.
- It should serve a useful function to the center. If not donated, the center would have had to buy it.
- It should be furnished directly to the center, and under the center's administrative control, rather than routinely provided as a public service as, for example, a public health visiting nurse.

For example, when a parent who works in an interesting place that charges an entrance fee to the public offers to get free admission for all the program's children, that is a donation. Its value will be the amount of the fees the center would have had to pay without the parent's offer. Include as donated services the dollar value of labor of all persons who provide specialized services to the center and who are qualified professional practitioners. Contributions of personal services can be computed on the basis of the value of the time contributed, whether at the minimum wage, or at the going rate in the community for the type of specialist donating the time in their specialization.

Public, tax-supported health services, such as free consultation from the nutrition or public health department of the state, are not donated services, since they are paid-for in another budget.

Additional Information on Staffing a Program

You will not be able to make your operating annual budget until you know precisely how many staff members you will pay and how much you will pay them for their level of knowledge and skill. The following are some tips on planning your staffing.

Expect peak enrollment the first week in September. If you staff for this peak time, you may be overstaffed the rest of the year. You will do better to cover this peak period by paying overtime and hiring temporary staff members. In an existing program, examine its past monthly enrollment figures to detect the year-round staffing pattern you will need.

If your center is open 9 hours or more per day, you will schedule staff to cover each room throughout the long day. You do this by *staggering work shifts,* and *adding part-time workers, as necessary.* Staff qualifications are specified by the Department of Education for schools; by the Head Start Bureau for Head Start; and by the licensing agency, for all private centers, both for-profit and not-for-profit. As an executive, you will have your own ideas of the kind of staff you want.

You will find a sample salary scale on the next page. This scale rewards staff for staying at the center (not cost of living), and also for increasing their professional qualifications through training. This scale applies to **Fairchild teachers, lead teachers, and curriculum specialists. The center developed separate scales that apply to its Director, to aides and assistant teachers, and to non-teaching staff.**

Some states' licensing rules define two different levels of teacher qualification. The states call the more qualified teachers by names like lead teacher, master teacher, and supervising teacher. Being in shorter supply, the more highly qualified teachers receive higher salaries. In those states,

Fairchild Development Center Salary Scale for Teaching Staff 1996

PAID EXPERIENCE	A NO FORMAL TRAINING	B UP TO 30 CREDITS	C AA DEGREE	D BA NOT ECE; OR AA ECE	E BA IN RELATED FIELD	F BA ECE	G BA ECE + 15 CREDITS	H MA ECE
Up to 1 year Experience	$14,300	$15,000	$15,600	$16,200	$16,800	$18,000	$18,800	$19,600
1-2 years Experience	15,264	15,900	16,576	17,172	17,808	19,080	19,928	20,760
2-3 years Experience	16,180	16,854	17,528	18,202	18,866	20,224	21,124	22,020
3-4 years Experience	17,150	17,866	18,580	19,284	20,010	21,428	22,394	23,240
4-5 years Experience	18,180	18,938	19,694	20,452	21,211	22,724	23,735	24,740
5-6 years Experience	19,270	20,074	20,846	21,680	22,482	24,088	25,058	26,220
6-7 years Experience	20,426	21,278	22,218	22,980	23,822	25,434	26,688	27,800
7-8 years Experience	21,652	22,554	23,456	24,259	25,670	27,066	28,268	29,800

Each step beyond the 8th step is an increase of 6% of the previous step. Experience must be at the Fairchild Center, except for the initial hire.

teachers are motivated to achieve the higher qualification by the potential for a higher salary. Many centers pay for college training for staff members so that they can become more qualified, whether or not the state requires it.

Each room's qualified person can be assisted by someone who meets qualifications to be an aide or assistant, and who can be in training to become a teacher later. It is common practice for centers to have two staff persons in the room: either a pair of team teachers, or a teacher and an assistant.

Small groups work best. Good children's programs create a feeling of community among children, staff and parents. That bonding is a part of their magic; it is what makes them good. It is difficult or impossible to develop such community in large groups. Groups of more than 20 children are too large for children ages four and five. Children ages three and under need even smaller groups.

For a center that is open 8 or 9 hours a day, and has two staff members at all times, you will need to employ 2.75 or 3 staff members per group to cover the day. You do this primarily by staggering the work hours to make sure the classroom is covered at both ends of the day. Sometimes a very valuable staff member will want a part-time job for a few years, which may help with your scheduling; but too many part-time solutions may undermine the continuity and feeling of community at the center. Staffing a children's program requires fine tuning and creative deployment of staff. You will need to staff your center room-by-room and person-by-person.

There is no sure-fire magic formula for staffing a room. Plan each room, group-by-group, so that you are assigning staff to meet ratio requirements throughout the day. That plan will determine how many and what staff are assigned to each room. At any given time, you will need enough staff on hand to respond to the needs of the individual children who are there, and to facilitate their becoming a group. Note that the ratios/group size criteria for accreditation by the National Association for the Education of Young Children (NAEYC), presented on page 204, represent a broad consensus on staffing necessary for quality.

As you plan the schedule for the program, remember that the staff who work with children will need time out of the classroom to plan, and remember that they have a legal right to break times, in addition to lunch.

More and more, as you try to put together the mosaic of staff and children that will implement your ideals, you will find yourself thinking in terms of individuals, and not formulas. Quality depends on who these people are — children as well as staff — and how they relate to each other.

Wage and Hour Laws

Make sure you understand how Wage and Hour Laws apply:

- Staff must be paid for the hours they work. No employee can work 40 hours or more in any week unless she is compensated. Hours in excess of 40 must be compensated at a time-and-a-half rate. If the Department of Labor determines that you have violated these rights of employees, you will have to make substantial back payments.

- The concept of "compensatory time" does not apply to any employee covered by Wage and Hour laws, unless it is used within the same workweek and is less than 40 hours.

- If the employer requires the employee to do anything, the employee must be paid for the time spent doing it. This includes training, conferences, and parent meetings. For example, if the Center requires an Assistant Teacher to take a course in order to do her job better, the Center Director must pay for the course, and for the hours spent taking it. However, if the employee is taking the course because the employee aspires to become a Lead Teacher (or achieve any role advancement), then the Center Director is not required to pay for the time or the course. In that case, the employee is not required by the employer to take it, and the benefit is to the employee rather than to the center.

- Audits may be routinely conducted by government or can be initiated in response to complaints by disgruntled employees. Wage and hour officials do not reveal to you whether or not there was a complaint.

Starting Up: The Initial Costs

A format for a start-up budget is shown on page 37. Starting a new children's program, or starting a new component added to an existing program, involves a number of costs that must be met before any operating money begins to come in. These costs include:

- Capital costs of building, land, and equipment.

- Human costs for planning, getting a program ready, securing a license, recruiting children and staff, and starting off with fewer children than capacity for the first several months.

- Lag costs, since there is a substantial time gap between providing the service and getting paid for it, particularly if government funds are involved. (You may have to pay your creditors before your debtors pay you.)

- Miscellaneous other costs, such as public relations; professional fees to lawyers, accountants and other consultants; and licensing, sanitation, and building approval fees and costs.

It is important to anticipate these costs as much as possible, to realize that they vary greatly, and to plan for a cushion against unanticipated costs. In addition to scrounging donated resources, the program will need some cash on hand to cover its operating expenses before income begins to flow.

Each of the line items in the start-up budget has a range of potential costs. At one extreme, you may not be making an expenditure at all. For example, if you find space that was previously used for a licensed children's program, you may not have to spend any money on renovation. Or you might feel you could get along with little or no staff training in advance of beginning the new program if money is tight and if you employ qualified staff. At the opposite extreme, the only space you can find may require extensive renovation, and you believe your staff needs extensive training.

You may meet some of your costs through contributions. Perhaps the person starting the program is an energetic parent, able and willing to donate time to the start-up activities. Perhaps you can get shelves, equipment, cubbies, and chairs built for much less than they would cost if you bought them ready-made. You may get some useful donations from individuals or groups willing to support one-time-only capital costs.

Form for a Start-Up Budget for a Child Center

Date, from _____ to_____

INCOME

Bank loan _____

Capital gifts and contributions _____

Fund raising events _____

Other _____

TOTAL INCOME $ _____

EXPENDITURES

	CASH	IN-KIND	AMORTIZE
Personnel			
Person who plans and implements start-up	_____	_____	XXXXXX
Staff employed before children are enrolled	_____	XXXXXXX	XXXXX
Fringe benefits @_____%	XXXXXXX	XXXXXXX	XXXXX
Contract services/consultants			
Architect	_____	_____	
Lawyer	_____	_____	XXXXX
Contractor	_____	_____	_____
Other	_____	_____	_____
Supplies	_____	_____	_____
Occupancy prior to enrollment			
Rent or mortgage	_____	_____	_____
Utilities	_____	XXXXXXX	XXXXX
Deposits	_____	XXXXXXX	XXXXX
Equipment and vehicles	_____	_____	XXXXX
Training of new staff	_____	_____	XXXXX
Board or parent meetings	_____	_____	XXXXX
Other			
License fee	_____	XXXXXXX	XXXXX
Insurance	_____	XXXXXXX	XXXXX
Publicity	_____	_____	_____
Payment into cash reserve	_____	_____	_____
Other	_____	_____	_____
TOTAL CASH NEEDED	$ _____	$ _____	$ _____

You can push a few of your initial costs into your first year's operating budget by paying some of your bills after the money starts to come in. The more you do this, however, the more you inflate your operating costs beyond the point that annual income can sustain them. You can amortize some costs over a longer period of time, such as a leasehold improvement that a landlord made and charged to you as part of the rent. Your accountant can help you identify options.

Early care and education administrators are known to be skilled mobilizers of people and scroungers of resources. At no time are these talents more needed than during the start-up period. Many people and resources in the community will need to be involved, in most cases, before the program gets off-the-ground, its license in-hand, its building equipped, and its finances under control.

Start-Up Details

Personnel costs: You will decide who is responsible for each start-up activity, whether it is a volunteer or a paid person. In large urban areas, it can take six months to a year to get a new children's program incorporated, building-approved, licensed and ready to operate. In other areas, the process may be faster. Even if someone is working without being paid during the initial start-up time, it must be decided at what point the paid director starts to work or, in the case of an owner-operated proprietorship, how long the owner can finance the program out-of-pocket before the program receives any income. Three months, if possible, is a reasonable time period, depending on the geographic area.

Most administrators starting a new program would like to employ a full staff, and train them as a team before any children enter. In practice, however, they usually compromise this ideal in the interest of cost feasibility. Cautious operators phase in new staff as they phase in new children, allowing for unanticipated delays in enrollment of children. Programs seldom reach their full capacity in a short time. Decisions about the number of staff to be employed before there are children, and the timing of hiring, will seriously affect start-up costs.

A Practical Note: **If feasible, it is desirable to pay one teacher/caregiver for each children's room three weeks before opening.**

Contract Services and Consultants: You may employ a lawyer to help with incorporation, tax status, and other legal aspects of start-up. Such help could cost you at least $250, probably more. Free or reduced cost legal help might be available from a Legal Services agency, a parent or friend. However, legal counsel is not an area where you should consider cost above quality. Legal aspects of starting your business are very important; you don't want to skimp on your lawyer.

In cities, you might be required to submit plans for building safety approval and zoning, for which you will need to hire an architect. These services can cost you several hundred dollars, but are not usually required in smaller communities. As you plan your start-up, you may need to budget for help from educators, doctors, nutritionists, psychologists, or other child experts, if you might need them before you start your program.

Supplies: Once your program is under way, supplies become an operating expense. You may want to purchase, at bulk rate, more supplies than you can use right away. In any case, your purchase expense is probably going to be greater when you start than it will be in subsequent months and years. If you defer major supply purchases to the point when the center is almost ready to begin, and spread some purchases over the year, you can avoid major start-up costs for supplies, and probably make wiser purchases. If you have adequate financing for start-up, you may want to finance some supplies up front as part of start-up, but you may also want to leave some decisions about purchases until you have a chance to operate for a while.

Occupancy: You will want to start occupying your building before you enroll children, in order to set up the rooms and get the building ready. Utility companies, the telephone company, your landlord, and other services may require deposits of various amounts before the program begins.

Selecting your building and site is probably the most important decision you will make. Your payment for rent or mortgage is buying you two things: a place to run your program, and advertising. *Remember:* **Occupancy costs are a combination of space and advertising. There are some locations where you will never break even.**

Before selecting the location, you will gather all the information you can find on: other community resources that can help the families you want to serve; competing children's programs; families' expressed preferences about types of child care, parents' patterns of travelling to work; and on parents' ability to pay. A well-located program, in an area of unmet demand, that is visible in the community, will reach and maintain its break-even point much more readily than a program that is not well-located and visible, or a program starting up in an area where parents are not seeking center care.

Besides deciding where to locate your program, you will have to decide whether to build, renovate, or find an existing program that needs no renovation, such as a former school, child care center, or hospital. You will also decide whether to own the building and make mortgage payments, or whether to rent. Construction and renovation costs might be $100 - $125 per square foot.

All these decisions have different cost implications, and you may need to pay for expert advice. Remember that your operating budget will not be able to sustain costs of occupancy if they represent too large a proportion of your overall costs. In general, children's programs are labor intensive, and your largest expense will be direct service staff.

In most states you will be required by center licensing requirements to have at least 35 square feet of usable space for each child. Most centers meet this requirement with 60% of their space, using an additional 40% of space for storage, kitchen, offices, hallways and adult meeting space. You can figure on needing at least 40% more space than the 35 square feet that is usable per child.

To determine the square footage you must have, multiply the number of children you expect to enroll by 35: that will give you the minimum square footage you need for 60% of your building. The calculation of total space needed, at a minimum, would be:

$$\frac{35 \text{ sq. feet}}{60\%} = \frac{X}{100\%} \qquad \text{or } .6x = 35 \text{ sq. feet} \qquad \text{or } X = 58.33 \text{ sq. ft./child}$$

In other words, 58.33 sq. ft. multiplied by the number of children you expect to enroll equals the total square feet you are required to have. You will probably want more.

These are minimum figures for the building alone, of course, and an ideal program would have at least 1000 square feet per child, including the entire land area. To determine your total building cost, estimate the number of square feet you want to have for the number of children you want to include; multiply it by square footage costs for building or for renting buildings in the local area you are considering, such as $100 per square foot.

The total land area for a 60-child center has been estimated at no less than 250 square feet per child, including all building space, outdoor play areas, driveways and sidewalks. A center for 120 children would require at least 500 square feet. If you can estimate the average cost of land per square foot, you can estimate the cost of the property you need. For example, if an average land cost were $1 per square foot, it would cost you $500 multiplied by 120 for land to build a center with 120 children, or $60,000.

Renovation costs vary from nothing or very little, all the way to close to the cost for new construction. If the building has not previously met a building code for a licensed children's program, a school, hospital, or similar use, it is likely changes will have to be made to meet requirements for building safety approval and for sanitation approval, both prerequisites for a license. These changes are likely to include protection for the furnace or boiler, additional exits, fire resistant doors, and kitchen and bathroom equipment. A wood frame house might require extensive renovation to make it safe for groups of children. A single-width storefront might cost at least $10,000 to renovate for 25 children.

Where there is a Housing Authority or Redevelopment Authority in the city or town, it is sometimes possible to get rent-free space for children's programs. However, public housing space may not meet licensing requirements. For example, there may not be two exits from each floor. Churches have classrooms that are often used only on Sunday, and that may not require much renovation. There are no hard and fast rules, but it is usually unwise to spend much more than $20,000 to renovate an old building. Before spending anything on renovation, make sure you have the building inspected by a qualified building inspector.

If you are renting the building, and the landlord makes the improvements you need, s/he can either charge you for them over a long period of time, or try to recapture them more quickly through high rent. In some cases, you can work with a friendly landlord to get the renovating done with volunteers. Since there are many ways landlords can handle these costs, you will want to discuss your financial situation quite fully with potential landlords, and find the landlord with whom you can develop the best working relationship.

Furniture, equipment, and vehicles: Some furniture and equipment is built in and amortized with the renovation costs. Equipment costs will vary widely. Initially, you will need equipment costs of $700 to $1000 per child, including kitchen equipment, educational equipment, office equipment, and other. You might have to budget even more to cover the cost of computer equipment, now under $1000, and ranging much higher. Playground equipment, to be safe, is expensive. Figure $50,000 - $98,000 for a medium-sized center.

More than half the start-up cost for equipment is likely to be spent on kitchen equipment. Initial expenses for kitchen equipment can easily run up to $10,000. Food money from the United States Department of Agriculture, administered by the Bureau of Nutrition in most states' Department of Education, may be available to cover kitchen equipment. With that possible exception, public funds are seldom available for equipment or other start-up costs, although government surplus equipment may be used. Sources of information about surplus equipment include the yellow pages, the licensing agency, the Department of Education.

Plan on 10% contingency for construction and renovation. Plan to operate at a deficit in Year 1 and Year 2.

Supplies: While supplies may be primarily in your operating budget rather than your start-up budget, you will need on hand, as you start out: $60 per FTE child, for teaching and learning materials; $20 per FTE child, for office supplies; and $40 per FTE child, for kitchen supplies.

Training: Your training plan will be affected by your decisions regarding phasing staff hiring. A new program may hire its core staff a little in advance of opening, bearing in mind that full staffing is not usually possible until enrollment is secure enough to justify it. An intensive orientation/training period the week before opening will help the staff operate as a team. However, even this is a costly practice for a center without access to much start-up capital.

Meetings: All expenses incurred in meetings of parents, planners, or staff; and all costs for transportation to visit other programs or go to meetings should be estimated. Staff time is paid time.

Insurance: You can probably include insurance costs in your operating budget, but they will be incurred before you begin. Shop around for the best price.

Publicity: Money spent on making a new program visible is worth the investment if it brings in more rapid enrollment. New programs usually have longer start-up periods than anticipated. It takes a long time before full capacity enrollment is reached. The longer the time, the most costly the operation and the more risky the endeavor. It is very important to use every creative way possible to let the community know of the new service and to build trust in its quality. You should set aside $100 per child for this outreach.

You will want an attractive sign, one that is in keeping with the style of the neighborhood in which you are locating. Your outdoor play equipment is a part of your attractiveness; however, you will have to assess the possibility of vandalism. Open houses; newspaper stories; flyers; and posters in supermarkets, photocopy stores, churches, and laundromats raise the level of community awareness of your program. An attractive Yellow Pages ad has been demonstrated to have a very high return. Mailings are expensive, but you can sometimes persuade your bank or other community merchant to include your flyer in one of their mailings.

Repayment of Loan: If you have borrowed money in order to start your center, you will include any interest payments in your operating budget. If you are able to repay the loan in the start-up period, include it as both income and expenditure in the start-up budget. If, as is more likely, you will be repaying the loan over a period of years, include the interest payments, but not the repayment of principle, in your operating budget. The principle is neither an operating cost nor a start-up cost. It will be included in your cash flow, and you will show it on your balance sheet. (See later sections on balance sheets and cash flow for more explanation.)

Cash Reserve: If you deal with government funds for the children participating in the program, you are almost sure to have a serious cash flow problem. It takes the government a long time to process your bills and reimburse your program for its expenses. Most likely you will have to pay the bills you owe, including your payroll, before the government pays you the money it owes you. It is necessary to have enough money on hand on opening day to cover your operating expenses for a while. The larger the percentage of your budget that is paid by government, the longer this cash reserve should stretch. Some experts say you need at least three months operating expenses in your start-up period, others say more, and some say less. You can offset some of these cash flow problems, and protect yourself against bad debts at the same time, by asking for a deposit of at least one week's fees from all your fee-paying parents. You can also charge an enrollment fee for families you accept and those on your waiting list. These sources for working capital help with cash flow.

Sources of Start-Up Funds

There is no government source of start-up capital, in most states. A few states have set up loan programs, or are encouraging the use of school buildings. Some parents can pay an initial deposit that will produce a little working capital. Most centers need to find start-up capital.

Not-for-profit programs usually seek their start-up funds through foundation grants or loans. Local foundations may be willing to help with start-up if they feel the program can demonstrate a capability to meet its operating costs after the start-up period. Individuals can make tax-deductible gifts to not-for-profit children's programs. Loans can be secured from individuals or from banks. In either case, the lender wants to know that the program will be able to repay the loan. Outright gifts, of course, are preferred to loans, which must be repaid.

Large for-profit corporations that operate children's programs have more options for recapturing start-up costs, in the sale of stock, real estate transactions, economies of scale for equipment, and management fees paid by employers for company-sponsored early care and education for employees' children. The small proprietor owning or running a local operation and the small for-profit corporation have fewer options. They can secure a loan from the Small Business Association (if for-profit) or from a bank. They can attract investors through adding equity to their own or someone else's investment in this start-up period.

Whether the needed cash is a loan or grant to a not-for-profit organization, or investment or a loan to a for-profit organization, it involves someone else's money. If a program does not appear likely to survive its start-up period, these outside funds are not readily available. Fifty percent of small businesses fail in the first two years. Bankers, investors, foundation executives understandably want to see evidence of sound financial planning before they part with their money. Of particular interest will be your ability to predict the point at which you are out of the start-up period, i.e., when you will break even.

Making a Financial Plan

An outline for a financial plan that would likely result in a loan or investment capital from a bank or individual is listed below. A proposal for a start-up grant would be similar in many ways. To emphasize the similarities, the outline describes what both would include. There would be differences in emphasis, with much more marketing information and strategy in a business plan, and more description of community needs and research findings in a proposal for funding. Both include:

Cover Sheet: Include the name of the organization, the address and phone number, and names of principal planners.

Table of Contents

Executive Summary: Include the amount of funds you need and your purpose for seeking them, as well as a brief summary of your plan. *(Write this last.)*

Section I.

Describe your organization, its capability, its mission, the experience and competence of the principals, and why it will be successful.

Section II. The Program

Detail what you want to do. Describe the legal form the program will take. Describe the target families that will use the program; the location selected; evidence of demand in the area; any competing services; the reasons for targeting the part of the market selected; how the loan, investment or grant will be used; its expected effect. Give the basics on the size of the program, and how it is organized. Present your view of your program's uniqueness, and the steps you are taking to assure the health, safety, and learning of children. This is a most important section for a foundation where the concern is for the value as well as the competence of the undertaking.

If your program is for-profit and you are seeking investors, you will have a separate section for a market analysis, and list it in the Table of Contents. If you are a not-for-profit seeking government help or loans from banks, you should include important marketing information in this Program section.

Section III. Financial Data

A. A budget, with sources of operating funds. Give a summary face sheet, followed by back-up detail; a start-up budget for a new program, with timetable for self-sufficiency; a request for funds, and a description of how they will be repaid, if you are requesting a loan.

B. Capital equipment list (omit for new programs)

C. Break-even analysis

D. Income projections
(Use budget face sheet, and project income for 3 years, in 3 columns)

E. Projected monthly cash flow for one year

F. Historical financial reports (existing programs only). Balance sheet for current year; add columns for past 3 years, if available.

Section IV. Management Summary

Organization chart, job descriptions, benefit package, training and retention strategies, recruitment strategies. Risk reduction and loss prevention, insurance coverage. Timetable and identification of persons responsible.

Section V. Supporting Documents

Add resumes of key personnel, letters of reference, copies of leases, contracts, licensing status, and anything else relevant to the plan; tax returns for for-profit organization; tax exempt documentation for not-for-profits; evidence of liability insurance coverage; news clippings.

Most children's programs are managed by directors who have had little practice in using the above financial reports themselves, much less demonstrating their competence to bankers and other sources of funds. Some of this information, such as the balance sheets in Section III.F above, will be prepared for you by your accountant, but much of the information is very future-oriented, and should be prepared primarily by the director, who is responsible for the future.

Assuming that the program has been able to secure start-up funds, and has its operating budget under good control, its director will need financial planning tools to keep it in good working order. Any new director entering a program and seeking to understand and guide its future will need these tools as well.

The remainder of this handbook is geared to helping children's program administrators master the basic useful tools for preparing and presenting information essential to a program's survival and quality.

3 The Income Side of the Budget

It should be clear after creating a line-item operating budget and a start-up budget that all budgets consist of two balanced sides: the money coming in and the money going out. The totals for each of these two sides must be equal for the program to survive. It is the job of the director, manager, administrator, executive, or leader to make sure they stay in balance.

If more money goes out than comes in, this leader is responsible for increasing income, reducing expenditures, or some combination of the two. In order to take timely action, the leader must know what is happening with the finances, and must know it in time to act on the knowledge. This handbook describes some of the basic tools that directors use to generate knowledge of what is happening.

Income is always related in some way to the number of children enrolled in the program. If the center gets a government subsidy, it is usually for purchasing care, or a grant, for a specified number of children. If parents pay fees, the amount of fees collected is related to the number of children enrolled. If the government has a sliding fee policy for its subsidy, then the parent fee plus the government subsidy for each child should add up to the per child cost of the program. If not, the program should make clear to the community that the organization is also subsidizing the child.

Utilization Factor

In the simple case of a children's program financed entirely by parent fees, the entire income side of the budget is based on the numbers of children and the fees paid for each of them. In your first planning of a budget, you are likely to simply multiply the expected number of children to be enrolled by the fees their parents will pay. However, that would be a serious mistake in planning. You would be overestimating income, and your planned expenditures would be greater than the income that actually does come in. You need to determine a *utilization rate,* or *utilization factor.*

Unless you over-enroll, it is not possible to operate your program at 100% enrollment. When children leave, others will not always take their place on the same day. A well-run center operates at 95% enrollment or above, but few programs achieve a utilization rate as high as 98%. Directors try to keep their utilization above 90% in a variety of ways, such as:

- careful attention to attendance records, being watchful that non-attendance not turn into non-enrollment;
- quick action to fill empty slots from a waiting list; and
- active recruitment activities to build good community relations even when all slots are filled.

To anticipate income accurately, do not expect 100% enrollment. New programs seldom reach 80% in the first year. Income based on fees will be:

Number of children x fees per child x utilization rate

Your *utilization rate* is your best estimate of the percentage of full enrollment that is represented by the children who will actually be enrolled over the course of the year.

For example, if your maximum capacity were 50 children, and your fee were $400 per month per child, then the maximum you could earn in fees would be $400 x 12 (months) or $4800 per year for each of the 50 children you plan to enroll.

If you budget to spend $4800 x 50, or $240,000, you will run out of money in May or June, or even sooner, because that is not really your expected earnings. If you are not a new program, you will be able to find your actual earnings in fees for the previous year. For example, perhaps last year you took in $229,150 in fees. Given the same capacity, you might assume that this figure is likely to be your income from fees this year too. If so, to get a utilization rate, divide the actual earnings, $229,150 by the maximum potential earnings $240,000. The resulting figure, .9573, is your utilization factor, expressed in a percentage as 95.7%.

If your utilization rate is lower than 92% after several years, you may not be monitoring enrollment to operate at an effective level, or you may not be letting the public know you are there.

The above example is a very simple one for a center operating entirely on parent fees, with no sliding fee scale, no part-time children, and no government subsidy or third party payer. Part-time children need to be estimated by adding them up to full-time equivalent children (FTE), in any way that reflects the fees charged them. In general, two half-time children will cost you more than one full-time child, and should be charged more than half the rate, to reflect your costs.

If parents pay a sliding fee, and the government pays the other portion of the sliding fee, the calculation can be made by combining both amounts paid into a total per-child fee, as follows:

Total fee income = # of children x (parent fee + govt. subsidy) x utilization rate

Fees Based on Enrollment vs. Attendance

Note that the calculation was again simple, because it was again assumed that parents were going to pay fees for all days, including holidays, illnesses, vacations and the like. It was further assumed that the policy of the government about paying you is the same as the policy of the parents.

These are reasonable assumptions, but they may be incorrect. They are reasonable because expenses of the center will continue on those days, so there is certainly a need for income to cover these expenses. Centers that charge on the basis of attendance, rather than enrollment, must cover these costs in another way, by charging high enough fees for the time the children attend to cover their costs for the days on which the children do not attend.

The calculations above assume that the center is charging a full fee for all weekdays, whether or not the child is there, with income based on enrollment, adjusted for actual enrollment rather than maximum potential enrollment. Probably the soundest policy would be to set fees in the expectation of a certain number of holidays per year, paid for staff, and a two week vacation for staff which is paid, with 2 week vacation for children which is not paid by the family. Most people can follow that pattern. The fees for the year would be great enough to cover the paid holidays for staff and the unpaid vacation of the children. The important point to make is that the center must know and plan its policy about enrollment, attendance, vacations and holidays when it determines its fees.

If the children's program is financed through government funds, state and/or federal policy will determine the basis for payment, whether enrollment, attendance, average annual enrollment, (as described above) or some other formula. States have policies that often penalize centers for periods of low attendance, as a way of promoting enrollment efficiency. Regardless of government policy, the budget used for management should project a true picture of expected fee income through use of utilization factor.

An alternative permitted in a handful of states is to over-enroll by the number of children expected to be absent, a practice which reduces the gap between enrollment and maximum enrollment at the same time that it increases the number of children in attendance.

Note that enrollment and attendance are not the same thing. A program can be fully enrolled and still go through periods of low attendance because of an influenza epidemic. No children's program, or any educational program such as a dancing class, a typing class, or a college course, can adjust its expenditures to reflect variations in attendance. Payment based on attendance destroys the stability of a program. Programs can and do base expenditures on expected enrollment, and adapt them to shifts in enrollment.

Another factor that affects income projections is bad debts, which vary from program to program. If your center has a history of bad debts, you will need to improve your fee collection procedures. Take into consideration your past experience of losses when you project income.

How to Enroll Full-time and Part-time Children without Losing Your Shirt
(Written by Beth Frederick and Gwen Morgan)

More centers are developing flexible enrollment policies that offer parents both full-time and part-time options. This practice can help the center budget, if done well, and can offer a service that customers need.

In a full-day program, the part-time child must be matched by another part-time child so that the "slot" or the "space" or "opening" is filled. For example, a morning child usually needs to be matched by an afternoon child. A child that comes Monday, Wednesday and Friday needs to be matched by a Tuesday/Thursday child. There are other combinations, and also solutions through staff who want to work part-time.

Centers should be careful about offering a half-day option within a full-day program, making sure they have staff who want to work half-time, and/or have plenty of free or low-cost space, or a customer wanting a matching option. Most centers will need to match-up a morning parent and an afternoon parent so they can pay their full-time staff and make full use of their space. Some programs have an afternoon school-age group using space that preschool children used in the morning: that use of space is efficient. It is complicated by the fact that public kindergartens often switch the same child from morning to afternoon sessions, and vice versa, during the year. Attending two different children's center programs can be over-stressful for some children.

Keep part-time spaces limited to a workable percentage of your total enrollment. It will be impossible to provide a good service if you spread yourself too thin. If you have spaces for 50 children, and convert them all to part-time, you could be trying to help 100 families or more. Your staff will not be able to tune-in on and know that many children and parents, and it is likely that the infant care will especially suffer.

You can convert a few spaces, possibly up to 20% of your spaces, to part-time, without this loss of quality. In part-day programs, 6 morning children can be matched up with 6 afternoon children. In part-week care, 5 children can be enrolled in 3 spaces, 10 in 6 spaces. Staff can be responsive to a few extra children and their families, but there must be a limit on the total part-time children.

Centers can't always give parents the exact days they request. You can offer parents a choice of a three-day pattern, or a four-day pattern, but a few of them may have to choose a pattern of days that you have designed. For example, you might set up three of your spaces to serve 5 families who want a three-day week:

Monday	Tuesday	Wednesday	Thursday	Friday
A	B	A	B	A
B	C	D	C	D
D	E	E	E	D

- Families A and D would enroll in Monday, Wednesday, and Friday.
- Family B would enroll in Monday, Tuesday, and Thursday.
- Family C would enroll in Monday, Thursday, and Friday.
- Family E would enroll in Tuesday, Wednesday, and Thursday.

You need to fill your slots according to your planned pattern in order to offer parents a cost-effective service. Your ability to accommodate to parents' workdays is somewhat limited.

If families seek four-day weeks, you could convert three openings to serve four families, three of whom would enroll in a four-day week (A, B, and C) with the other (D) enrolling in a three-day week, as follows:

Monday	Tuesday	Wednesday	Thursday	Friday
A	A	A	A	C
C	B	B	B	B
D	C	D	C	D

If you think your staff can be trained to do it well, you might want to consider drop-in care as an additional option. You would set aside a few spaces to be filled by drop-in children, and you would also have spaces available when enrolled children are absent. Drop-in care would be available only for a child whose parent calls in the morning and determines that there is room that day. As with part-day care, you would want to limit the availability of drop-in care to a reasonable number of enrolled families so children would know each other and staff could know the families.

A half-time child is not a half-price child. You need to consider your costs. A three-day option will necessarily be priced higher than 3/5 of a full day option.

Enroll children in groups, not just one at a time. Infant programs, in particular, tend to admit babies as they apply, rather than wait for a cost-effective group to form. This practice can be costly. If your center is fully enrolled, you can accept parents on a wait list for a part-time pattern, as described above. But if you do not find the other part-time parents to make it economically feasible, you will need to give priority to a full-time child for the "slot." Decide in advance how flexible you are going to be.

Be flexible during start-up. You can be a lot more flexible when your center is just starting than when you are fully enrolled with a wait list. During start-up a center needs to fill every space as rapidly as possible. For example, a center can enroll a child in a Monday, Wednesday, and Friday pattern, even without finding the other families in the pattern, if the alternative is to leave the space unfilled. However, the parent can be told, in writing, "We can enroll you in this pattern from now until next November 1, but this particular three-day option may not be available after that date." The agreement with the family can be time-limited.

Monitoring Enrollment and Attendance

There are many ways of anticipating income and expenses in relation to numbers of children: attendance, enrollment, average attendance, or average annual enrollment. Many states, unfortunately, reimburse on the basis of attendance, and many parents would like to pay by attendance.

Children's programs that operate in crowded urban areas, with long waiting lists, are not likely to have a major recruitment problem, but they will have to keep careful track of attendance to be sure a child has not dropped out without the director's knowledge. Someone should be examining attendance records weekly. Since the income projection is based in one way or another on the number of children, every child lost will mean a serious reduction in income.

The number of children per staff person (ratio) is a central factor in children's programs' expenditures. If you have budgeted for twelve three-year-olds and two caregiver/teachers, and decide to accept an extra child, you will find yourself with plenty of leeway to buy what you need all that year. If, on the other hand, you have budgeted for twelve three-year-olds, but can only enroll eleven children, you will be losing money rapidly and endangering the whole program. Cutting the paper napkins in half and watering the poster paints will not help at all. The financial problem lies in the ratio. One child will make a tremendous difference. Whenever a child leaves, every week that goes by without filling the space is a threat to the program's survival.

In less densely populated areas, monitoring attendance to assure continuing enrollment is even more critical. With a less substantial pool of children from which to draw compared to urban areas, the program may be faced with extinction, particularly in times of recession, as families lose their jobs and cannot continue to pay for a space. It becomes vital to keep the entire community aware of the program's existence and to use every public relations technique possible to be sure that the entire pool of families in the area, and their employers, know about the program.

In rural areas, where population is thin, a children's program will need to place greater emphasis on inclusion and multi-purpose services in order to fill its openings within a reasonable commuting distance. In such areas, the children's program serves a wide range of needs because the area cannot support specialized separate programs for different needs.

It is clear that attendance records, combined with fee records, are among the most important of financial management records. The information they contain should be examined frequently, and acted upon at once. Sample forms for recording monthly and weekly attendance and fees follow on the next pages.

Recruitment of Children

Recruitment of children is almost synonymous with good community relations. Public relations, mentioned earlier in the section on start-up budgets, will be an ongoing need for any program that does not have a self-generating waiting list. Even with a waiting list, many programs still make efforts to be visible, as a hedge against shifting economic conditions of the future and as a way of educating the community to the service they offer and the reasons for its price.

Monthly Record of Attendance and Fees

Date _____

Name of child	M	T	W	Th	F	Fee	M	T	W	Th	F	Fee

1 = Sent first notice after 1 week in arrears
2 = Sent second notice one week later
3 = Sent termination warning one week later
4 = Sent termination notice one week later

M	T	W	Th	F	Fee	M	T	W	Th	F	Fee	1	2	3	4

Weekly Summary of Attendance, Amounts Due and Cash Receipts

Name of Child	Attendance					Amt. Due This wk.	Previous Balance	Rec'd This wk	Due Next
	M	T	W	Th	F				

Explanation of adjustments in amount due this week.

Center Director's

Signature _____

Week Ending _____

Social Worker's

Signature _____

Deposit Date _____ No. _____

White=Finance Copy   Canary=Center Copy   Pink=Audit Copy

Some programs depend on recruiting parents who can afford to pay; others have contracts with the state for children eligible for subsidy; some are sponsored by employers or by churches. Regardless of who pays, it is a good idea for children's programs to make sure that the families in the community know of the program, rather than relying only on a funding source that may not be able to keep the spaces filled. You cannot afford to let much time go by with unfilled spaces in your program if you are counting on those fees in the income side of your budget. It is better to use all ways you can to be known in the community.

Reaching Out

Almost every community has a resource and referral (R&R) agency that informs parents of their choices, and how to choose. Since these R&Rs speak with parents all the time, they can give you a good idea of what parents are looking for and whether they are finding it. Your program should be listed at the R&R. Be sure the R&R knows and can tell parents anything unique about your program, such as accreditation, or an award you have earned. R&Rs do not choose for parents or make recommendations, but they can pass on factual objective information.

In addition to making sure the R&R knows about your program, you will want to take steps of your own to keep your service visible in the community. Even when you have a waiting list, you need this visibility to maintain good community relationships with sources of funds and loans. The best sources of recruitment do not cost much money although they do use valuable time. They include spending time on the telephone with parents seeking services, even when there is no room, in order to retain good will in the community.

The most common avenue used by consumers in choosing anything, and the most effective means of reaching consumers, is word of mouth. You want to make sure that the parents who use your program, and all their friends and relatives, think well of you, and that nobody in the community has a bad experience in relating to you. You can further promote word of mouth by visiting employers' personnel departments and letting them know how many employees of their company are enrolled in your program. You can also stimulate word of mouth with a feature story about your program in the newspaper or a magazine.

After word of mouth, the most effective method of recruitment of children is the Yellow Pages. An ad placed there has a much higher return than a classified ad placed in the newspaper. Another good and important method of outreach is the development and distribution of brochures, and giving them to real estate agents, pediatricians, people who visit your center, churches, libraries, health departments, R&Rs, schools, and above all to your parent group to distribute. Similarly, bright and creative flyers can be tacked up in the same places, and in supermarkets, laundries, and apartment complexes.

Someone in your program is sure to have an eye for artwork, clever formatting, and logo design. Your sign and your outdoor play area attract attention, and will silently recruit future children as yet unborn as their parents pass your program and find it appealing. You can extend this impact by having open houses and inviting the public. Your fundraising events, such as bake sales, fairs, children's movies, guest speakers, dances, musical entertainment and the like, can also be designed to appeal to and entice parents who might want to use your service. In the same way, you might develop a booth for the county fair, or a float for a local parade. Television and radio spots also help to get your story told.

Ask parents who enroll how they heard of your program. They will tell you what you are doing that reaches the most parents.

Waiting List Policies

Waiting lists are useful to the program as a pool from which to fill spaces, preventing a loss of time in recruitment of new children. They are also useful for documenting to the media, to funding sources, and to policy-makers in government a demand for expanded services in your area. For example, research has shown that families on the waiting lists earn less than those whose children are enrolled.

Wait lists are not a good indication of overall demand in a community, since parents may sign up for the wait list in several centers, while other centers in the community have unfilled spaces. Those centers with wait lists are likely to be those that parents perceive as high in quality.

All these uses for waiting lists are based on the expressed needs of parents and their children, rather than some hypothetical questions asked on a survey. Waiting lists are seen as valuable by parents as well. The existence of a waiting list implies that the program will be fair in admitting children as new spaces open up, and will not accept another family on an unfair basis. It is important that parents' expectation of fairness be taken seriously.

If some or all of the children in your program are subsidized, the government will probably have its own waiting list policies. You might have to accept eligible children for subsidy ahead of working parents who will pay. To many centers, that policy feels unfair. It is possible that you can apply the government criteria to a defined block of children (which for accounting purposes would be defined as a "program") while still offering spaces for children ineligible for subsidy but needy for the service. You will have to work out your own wait list policies within the constraints of government policy.

Now that government subsidizes a large number of children in Head Start, schools, and private programs, and now that need for children's programs is widely recognized, it has become increasingly important to have fair wait list procedures. The Constitution requires such fairness for the use of public funds, so that your use of public subsidy from tax dollars will leave you vulnerable to lawsuits unless your records indicate that you accept people from the waiting list into funded "slots" according to a fair and consistent policy.

One criterion viewed as fair is the time of application. Of two equally deserving families, it is fair to accept the one who applied first. If there are many families competing to get into the service, this policy could result in a long wait for everyone, in which case the service would be fair, but not especially helpful to anyone. No family can wait three years to get their child into an infant program for example. Some centers have their own priorities, and would accept a family in a dire emergency ahead of a family that has been waiting for a long time. Such a policy should be written down. When you are filling a space that is in demand by more than one person, you will need your own clear policy for all the spaces in your center, and policy for accepting children for whom the government is paying.

You should try to retain the right to balance groups by age, sex, and in other ways. That kind of consideration will determine whether a "slot" has opened up, and for whom. You cannot fill a space for a girl in your three-year-old group with a five-year-old boy; it is not that kind of "slot."

A "slot" is a space for a child in a program for a year. One "slot" might be filled by several children over the course of a year. It is an opening that is not specific to a particular child. A "slot" does not ever mean a child; it means a space that can be offered to a child. In general, this book uses the term "space" or "opening" to convey this meaning, but the term "slot" has a precise meaning in contracting with government.

If there are government policies for any priority acceptance into subsidized spaces, and you have a contract for a subsidized space (or spaces), you will have to follow those policies. If you receive public subsidy, there will be state policies on waiting lists for subsidized spaces.

To the extent possible, you will want to have some say in defining an opening. For example, you cannot fill an opening in the three-year-old group with a four-year-old. And if your center is becoming out-of-balance with more boys than girls, you will want to try to define the opening as an opening for a girl.

If children are to have continuity of relationships, they should continue in the same program that their parents chose, as long as they still want it and need it. Some states interrupt continuity as eligibility changes. If your state does not have a policy of "continuity" of services, then you could accept a subsidized family only to have to drop the child out of your program, or at least into an unsubsidized space, in order to admit a higher priority subsidized child.

As parents are placed on your waiting list, you should explain to them the conditions for deciding that a space is open, and the priorities for acceptance from the waiting list for that space. You should also explain to them your policy of dropping names from the waiting list. For example, if you drop names after six months, parents should know that. If you want to be extra fair, you can send postcards to those being dropped from the list. You ought not cut off the waiting list if parents want to be placed on it, but you can explain to them that there is little or no chance of their getting in when the list reaches a certain length.

Setting Parent Fees

Fee setting is based on a complicated set of decisions. You might set your fees based on what parents can afford to pay (about 10% of their family income if they are at the median income). Alternatively, you might set fees based on the "going rate" in the community. Either way, you may not generate enough income to cover the costs of operating the kind of program you want. You may be forced to subsidize the parents through underpaying your staff, accepting as a given the very low salaries offered in child care programs. If you set your fee based on your costs, including reasonable salaries for your staff, you may charge considerably more than the "going rate" and you may fail to enroll many parents.

In the section on "break-even analysis" that follows, you will find further information and methods that will help in computing fees. Your first consideration should be to establish your total fee for a space for a year in your program. Regardless of whether the parent pays the whole fee, or it is made up of parent fees + third party payments, you need to be paid a fair per-child fee for the service.

Many children's programs are trying to find ways for parents to pay what they can afford, on a sliding fee scale. In a few communities, United Way supplements parents' fees on a sliding fee basis. Some states pay the part of a fee that parents cannot afford to pay. A few employers supplement what their employees pay through a voucher system. Some centers have their own sliding fee scale. The basic thing to remember is that when parents pay what they can afford, rather than the cost, somebody else has to pay the difference between what the parent can pay and the cost of the service to the center.

A sliding fee scale can be expressed in dollars, determining how much the parent can be expected to pay, and how much somebody else would have to pay. Another approach is to have a sliding percentage of income that parents have to pay. The percentage would become greater as income rises. Either way, it should be clear that parents at the poverty income level cannot pay very much, since all their income is used up in taxes, food, and shelter.

Most sliding fees assume that the full fee paid by the parent who is charged the highest rate is the actual cost of the service. Lower fees are like scholarship aid, helping the parents who cannot pay the full cost. Some not-for-profit programs have tried setting the top fee, or full fee, higher than the cost of the service, in an effort to have the high-income parents subsidize the lower-income parents. This "Robin Hood" kind of fee schedule is not usually acceptable to parents. The full cost of the service is so great that, while there are some, very few parents would willingly pay even more to help out families with less ability to pay.

There are also federal tax credits that help out parents who pay for child care. The following chart shows the dollar amounts of the federal child care credit that is available to parents at different income levels. Some states have tax credits too.

MAXIMUM FEDERAL DEPENDENT CARE TAX CREDITS

ADJUSTED GROSS INCOME	PERCENTAGE	ONE CHILD OR DEPENDENT	TWO OR MORE DEPENDENTS
Up to $10,000	30%	$720	$1,440
10,001 - 12,000	29%	696	1,392
12,001 - 14,000	28%	672	1,344
14,001 - 16,000	27%	648	1,296
16,001 - 18,000	26%	624	1,248
18,001 - 20,000	25%	600	1,200
20,001 - 22,000	24%	576	1,152
22,001 - 24,000	23%	552	1,104
24,001 - 26,000	22%	528	1,056
26,001 - 28,000	21%	504	1,008
28,001 and over	20%	480	960

Centers should inform parents how to apply for the federal tax credit, and also how to get their withholding tax adjusted so that they have the money to pay for their child care on payday instead of having to wait for a reimbursement at the end of the year. A drawback of using the withholding mechanism is the "use it or lose it" provision. However, the cost of a children's program is very predictable, with little danger that the parents would end up owing more taxes than they expected at income tax time. On pages 64 and 65, you will find a handout for parents on the tax credit. Before handing it out, check to be sure that Congress has not made changes to the information mentioned.

Another important source of federal tax assistance to parents is the **Earned Income Tax Credit.** This credit goes to low-to-moderate income families with a child, when one of the parents is working. Many of these families do not earn enough to have to file tax returns, but the E.I.T.C. is a refundable credit, which means that if the parent owes no taxes, but is eligible for the credit, the Internal Revenue Service pays the credit to the family. There is no requirement that the family spend their money on children's programs.

Parent fees, therefore, are already federally subsidized by tax credit, with more tax help for families that earn less. But the tax provisions can only help families who know how to apply for a credit and receive it.

Collecting the Fees

Most children's programs, whether for-profit or not-for-profit, end up at some time or other providing a service for parents who simply cannot pay for it. There are heart-rending cases that directors have not been able to turn away, at least for a while. On the other hand, the program itself will fail, and all the other families will lose their valuable service, if the fees the program depends on are not collected. All administrators face this dilemma.

The successful administrators, whose programs survive, report that they are firm, consistent, and quick to follow-up in their fee collection processes. The less successful administrators are those with relaxed procedures that let a parent get too far into debt before they try to catch up with the situation. It is not humanitarian to place parents under the stress of piled-up debt. From the perspective of parents, as well as of administrators, clear policies with frequent follow-up are important.

Fee collecting is so time-consuming that it adds considerably to administrative costs unless serious attention is given to streamlining the procedures themselves. When parents are permitted to pay at any time of the week, the time that requires of the program staff adds up. If parents all pay on the same day, one staff person can handle the whole procedure in one part of the day, and get the money to the bank where it will be safe with a minimum of wasted effort. It is therefore desirable to ask parents who pay by check, through the mail, to send the payments before a specified time, and to ask those who pay in person and in cash to do so only on one specific day each week.

To record the cash payments, you should use a numbered receipt book with carbon copies, which will enable you to have a record on file as a crosscheck for your attendance and fee record. Your deposit slip for the bank should list the names of those who paid, and this slip can be photocopied for your files.

Parents' Questions about the Federal Dependent Care Tax Credit

A Handout Factsheet

If you spend money on child care you can get between 20% and 30% of what you spend, depending on your income, taken out of the tax bill you owe the federal government at income tax time. Only up to $2400 for an only child or $4800 for more can be claimed.

WHO CAN GET THE TAX CREDIT?

You can qualify if you:

✔ work for pay, part-time or full-time, or are searching for employment.

✔ do not earn less than you pay for child care (either spouse).

✔ have one or more children under age 15 for whom you are entitled to a personal exemption.

✔ are a single person, or have a spouse who also works or is a full-time student 5 months of the year, or is disabled.

WILL THE CREDIT APPLY TO ALL MY TAXES?

No. The credit applies only to your federal income tax. Some states, but not all, have a deduction or a credit for state tax.

DO I HAVE TO WAIT UNTIL THE END OF THE YEAR TO GET THE CREDIT?

No. The credit can increase your paycheck so you can have the money to spend on your child care IF you claim it by filling out the W-4 withholding form.

WHAT CHILD CARE EXPENSES CAN BE COUNTED?

Everything you have to spend on child care so you can work counts, except:

- anything above $2400 for an only child and $4800 for all your children.

- costs of transportation from home to care.

- child care expenses that are greater than what you earn if you are single, or greater than what the lowest paid

WHAT PERCENT OF MY EXPENSES MAY I SUBTRACT FROM MY TAX?

If your annual income is under $10,000 your credit is 30% of what you spent on child care. For every $2000 you earn above $10,000, deduct 1% from the credit, up to $28,000 at which point the credit remains 20%.

WHAT TYPE OF CHILD CARE COUNTS?

Payments you make to centers, nursery schools, family child care providers and babysitters in your home.

WHAT IF MY CHILD IS SUBSIDIZED?

If government or somebody else pays part of your child care, you are not spending money on that, and therefore cannot claim a credit for your costs. But if you pay anything, you can claim that part of the care that you have to pay for.

HOW DO I CLAIM THE CREDIT?

When you file your income tax on Form 1040 or 1040A, you must attach to it the Form for Credit for Child and Dependent Care Expense (Form 2441). On it you must itemize your child care expenses. You should have receipts for those expenses in your files.

CAN I PAY MY RELATIVES?

Not unless they are your employees, for whom you are withholding Social Security taxes, or if they work for another organization that provides child care, and not if they are your dependents.

HOW DO I GET MY PAY CHECK INCREASED?

Fill out a W-4 form with your employer. List what you pay for child care per week, multiply that by the number of weeks you will use child care. This annual expected cost can then be multiplied by the percent of credit that you are entitled to, up to the limits. A table on the form will help you decide the number of allowances you should claim, usually *more than the number of dependents*. When you do this, you are telling the government that you will not be owing them a certain amount of tax money, and therefore it will not be taken out of your salary to pay the taxes you owe. But if you overestimated, you'll have to pay the government later, so be careful.

Sources of Funds for Children's Programs

The sources of funds for children's programs fall into four categories: parent fees, government subsidy, employers, and private charity.

It is possible, but not easy, to run a program that is financed entirely with parent fees. Without other sources of support, a center cannot pay the wages its staff deserve, and has difficulty achieving quality. Parents can receive help from government and from their employers, via deductions and credits on their tax returns.

Some work-related centers are substantially supported through employers. Either a single employer or a collaboration of employers can support a program in many ways. Such a center might have per-child support for a liberal budget, approved by the employer, particularly paying noticeably higher staff benefits than community-based programs. In addition, the employer may be willing to pay a management fee of $60,000 or more to the organization running the children's program. There could be in-kind services offered by an employer or employers. Through their Dependent Care Assistance Programs, employers can help to create a tax-free benefit for their employees.

Government sources of support will vary a great deal with time, although working with government is similar even when funding sources change. The major sources of funds in 1999 will no longer be the major sources of funds in 2004. Current sources include:

The Public Education System: Funds to support programs that include children with special needs of all ages, also pre-kindergarten programs, usually part-day, usually run by local schools.

U.S. Department of Agriculture, primarily through state Departments of Education: Food subsidy for children's programs.

Head Start: Federal funds for low-income children, with standards of quality. When Head Start funding expands, new grantees can apply. Infant programs in Head Start are expanding. Funding is a grant. Low-income eligibility inhibits its potential for working parents.

TANF Child Care: Temporary Assistance to Needy Families, administered by state Welfare Departments, as part of Welfare Reform, to reduce welfare dependency. Often funded through voucher program.

Child Care and Development Block Grant (CCDBG): A major federal support for early care and development programs, primarily full-day. Has been folded together with *At-Risk* child care, a welfare-related source, but since CCDBG is 100% federal and has no matching requirements, the two retain their separate identity to some extent. Funding is usually by contract or voucher, a parent-choice mechanism.

State Funds: Some states have appropriated state tax dollars to pay for some of their child care costs, often combining state with federal dollars.

Break-even Analysis

The concept of break-even is well expressed in the word "break-even." When the expenditures are the same as the revenues, an organization breaks even. Any new organization can expect the budget not to break even at first, before it has sold a certain number of products, or, in the case of child care, enrolled a certain number of children. Obviously it is very important to try to predict when the budget will break even: at what price? at what point in time? at what number of enrolled children?

If you know your break-even point, you know when you will be able to begin repaying any loans you have taken out. This information is usually much more valuable than your net worth, to you and to your bank.

Break-even analysis is also very important as a way of determining how to price your services. **If the price is too low, you will never break even. The more children you enroll, the more money you lose.** Alternatively, in a situation where a program has a fixed fee already, such as a reimbursement rate from the state, a break-even analysis will enable you to determine how many children you must enroll before you break even.

To break even is to reach the point where income and expenditures exactly balance. The concept is especially important when a new program is starting up, and you are deciding what number of children to enroll or what fees you will charge, and when you will begin to break even. It helps you to understand how long you might operate at a loss, or how much cash reserve you need before you turn the break-even corner. When you add new program components (such as infant care or after-school care) to an existing service, break-even analysis again becomes useful as you navigate the new start-up.

If your program is already in operation, and the size of the groups and fees are stable from year to year, a break-even analysis is useful only if you want to rethink the number of children or the fees charged in any or all of the groups. This might happen if the program is not doing well, or if it loses a stable source of outside funds.

In early care and education programs, break-even is especially useful when comparing different programs. Are you losing money on any of the programs? Do any of them make money for you that helps you to float other programs? A "program" for this purpose might be, for example, the infant/toddler program, the preschool program, the kindergarten, the after-school program, or the drop-in program, even though you think of your center as one whole program. Each of these examples has its own expenditures and might have its own fees, so that it can be thought of as a "program" for fiscal purposes.

The simple formula for break-even is:

$R = F + V$, where

R = Revenues

F = Fixed Costs, and

V = Variable Costs.

For a children's program, the left side of the equation can be made a little more complex. In the case of a program dependent on fees from parents and/or the government, R (revenues) can be considered to be NT, where

N = Number of children, and

T = Per child tuition or fee.

Therefore, your formula might be:

NT (the same as R) $= F + V$

You could solve the equation to find out either N (number of children to enroll) or T (price to charge).

To analyze your break-even point, start with the budget of the whole center. Divide the expenditure figures into two categories: fixed and variable.

Fixed costs are all the costs that stay the same, regardless of the number of children enrolled in your program. Examples include your space, director salary, insurance, heat, phone, snow plowing, etc. Use the accountants' principle of K.I.S.S. (Keep it simple, stupid!) and avoid all the "what if" issues, such as the fact that if you only had two children enrolled, you wouldn't be renting such a big building. Use the actual budget figures without obsessing over what-ifs.

Variable costs are all the costs that vary with the number of children enrolled in your program. Some vary exactly: one child, one sandwich; two children, two sandwiches; etc. Some vary with "clumps" of children, such as ratio cohorts. Those that vary with "clumps" of children can be called *semi-variable costs.* For example, once you have met the costs for a small group of 5 children, you do not add any costs when you add the 6th, 7th, or 8th child, but you might need another increase in staff costs when you add a 10th child.

Initially, in order to learn the break-even concept, concentrate on two categories, fixed and variable, including the semi-variable costs in the variable cost category.

Having separated these costs into fixed and variable for your entire center, you have already learned the essence of the break-even concept, and you can begin to apply it. Start with the assumption that every classroom must bring in enough revenues to cover its own share of total costs, fixed + variable. Figure out for your program what share of fixed costs each classroom must carry. To do that, you might divide the fixed costs by the number of classrooms in order to distribute the fixed costs equally across each classroom. Alternatively, you might figure what percent of the total children are in each classroom, and assign that percentage of fixed costs to that classroom. The information you seek is this: in each classroom, does the tuition paid for the children add up to the fixed-plus-the-variable costs for that classroom?

How to Do a Fast Break-even Chart for Each Classroom

1. Determine the fixed and variable costs for the center as a whole. Determine the variable costs for each classroom, and assign each room its fair share of the fixed costs.

2. On a sheet of graph paper, develop a horizontal axis across the bottom of the page, representing numbers of children, starting at 0 and continuing to the number of children in the group, and possibly 5 or 10 more children. The vertical axis (along the left side of the graph paper), representing dollars, starts at 0 and rises by $1000 or $10,000 increments, to the total tuition charged to the children enrolled in the group, and possibly another $10,000.

3. Calculate this classroom's share of the fixed costs, as described above.

4. Plot these fixed costs as a straight horizontal line on your graph, starting at the number of dollars on the left margin, and drawing a line straight from the left margin to the right margin.

5. Calculate the variable costs for this classroom. Place a dot on your graph above the number of children enrolled, and horizontally aligned with the dollars that represent the total budget, fixed + variable, for this classroom. (You are using the total because you are plotting a point that represents the fixed costs, already on the graph, plus the variable costs you are now adding.)

6. Draw a straight line from the left margin, the point where you plotted the fixed costs, through the dot you made in step 5, and continue this line to the far edge of the page.

7. Figure the revenues for this classroom as the number of children enrolled multiplied by the total per child fees paid by parents and third party payers like government. Make a dot representing this number of dollars, aligned above the number of children enrolled.

8. Draw a straight line through the dot you made in step 7, to the corner of the graph at the lower left, representing zero. Continue the line to the right side of the page.

9. Draw a circle around the break-even point, where the revenue line crosses the total cost line. If they never intersect, you are not breaking even.

After you have learned to make the first of these charts, you can make others very rapidly. If the income line never intersects the expenditure line, you never break even. That means the program is not self-sustaining, and not supporting its share of the fixed, as well as the variable costs. In that case, either you enroll more children, charge higher tuition, raise additional non-tuition funds, or subsidize this classroom from another classroom that more than covers its own share of fixed costs.

If you get in the habit of rapidly calculating your break-even point, classroom by classroom, you will get a feel for the way your program is working financially, and you will avoid the trap of looking only at the variable costs, and leaving your fixed costs unmet.

Quick Break-even Chart

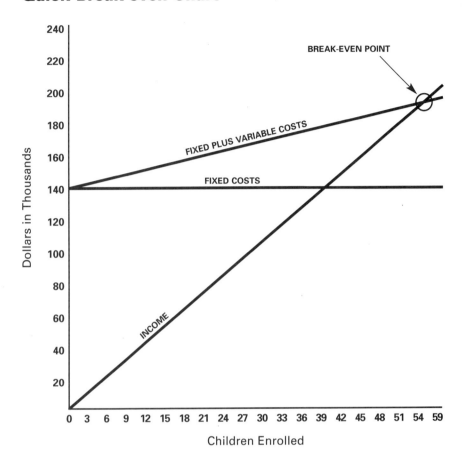

Break-even Charts as Visual Aids

Once you have mastered the break-even concept, and have learned to use it in your own calculations and as part of your thinking about classrooms breaking even, it can be used as a visual aid in presenting information to others about your center. Such a chart might be useful for many purposes, for example:

- demonstrating your competence to a banker or other source of capital;
- predicting when you will be able to repay a loan;
- demonstrating to parents why the current fees charged are not enough to break even;
- demonstrating to the board of directors the need for additional revenues.

You can use the simple, three-straight-line graph described above, or you can create a graph that shows the stair step-like way in which costs in educational programs really increase, not child by child, but by ratio or classroom "clumps" of costs.

Costs in an educational program do not all vary by each child. All the staffing costs will vary by ratios or by classrooms. That is, the staffing cost for one child is the same as that for two, or three, or four children, but at some point you will hire another set of staff members, and the cost will rise very steeply, then stay the same for another number of children. To make this graph, follow these steps:

1. Divide the entire budget into fixed, variable, and semi-variable costs. The semi-variable costs will be the teachers, assistant teachers, and substitutes, to cover all the hours the program is open. These semi-variable costs, remember, do not vary child by child; they vary by groups or "clumps" of children. Fixed costs are those costs that do not vary with enrolled children (Keeping It Simple, K.I.S.S.) The variable costs will be those costs that vary exactly in proportion to children enrolled, i.e., classroom supplies and food.

2. On a sheet of graph paper, draw a horizontal line across the bottom to plot numbers of children, using fives, eights, or whatever number fits with the ratios you are using. The line should go up to and beyond the number of children enrolled.

3. Now plot a vertical line down the left margin of the paper. Where the two lines meet is "0". This vertical line represents dollars. Plot by $10,000 or more increments, up to and beyond the total budget of the center.

4. Plot the fixed costs on the graph as a straight line from the left margin, at the appropriate number of dollars, straight to the right side of the page.

5. Plot your variable costs on top of the fixed costs. Do this by making a dot above the total number of children enrolled, aligned with the total variable costs. Draw a straight line through this dot to the top of the fixed costs on the far left. Keep the line going to the right edge of the paper.

6. Plot the first increment of semi-variable costs on the left axis. Determine the increment as follows. First determine how many "clumps" of children are in the center. The "clump" might be the

average ratio, at which you would add more staff, or it might be the average classroom size. Divide the total semi-variable costs by the number of "clumps." This gives you a "clump cost." Plot this cost on the vertical axis on the left, either by inches, or number of squares. This gives you the total of fixed + semi-variable costs. Note the length of this line; it must be the same every time you add the first child of another "clump."

7. This "clump cost" will remain the same until you have to add another clump of staffing costs. However, your line will not be a flat horizontal line because you are adding these "clump" costs on top of your variable costs line, which is a slanted one. You need to draw a line that parallels the slanted line of the variable costs, up to the point where you need to add another "clump."

8. Your second "clump cost" line will be the same length as the first one. The line that connects it to former and future "clump" costs will go straight up vertically. From here, you add a slanted horizontal line exactly parallel with and exactly the same length as the one you added horizontally at your first "clump cost."

9. Continue to add vertical "clump cost" lines and slanted connecting lines until you run out of graph paper.

10. Add your income line as follows. Make a dot representing the total revenues from the current number of enrolled children, aligning this dot with the dollars on the left vertical axis, and the number of children enrolled on the horizontal axis across the bottom. Connect this dot with a straight line to the "0" corner where your horizontal and your vertical axes meet. Extend this line to the top of the page.

11. Circle the "break-even points" where the income line crosses and then exceeds the total cost line. Determine which break-even point represents financial stability, i.e., you will break even and income will continue to exceed costs.

Of course if the center does not break even, you then need to make another chart or charts, presenting your idea of how it should be priced, or enrolled, so that it can break even. Instead of another chart, you might choose to give the comparable information in two colors on the same chart. For example you could have a chart with two income lines, representing two different tuition policies. You could plot the staffing costs in two colors, comparing two different ways of staffing the center.

Break-even Chart

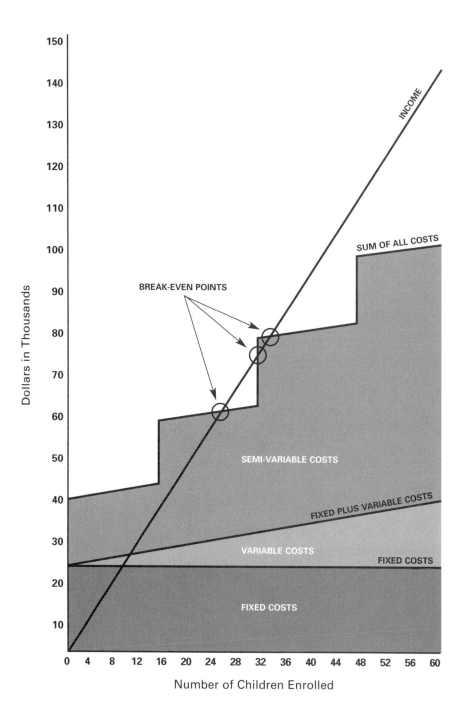

4 The Expenditure Side of the Budget

The starting points for understanding financial management are budgets. This book has presented a start-up budget and an annual operating budget to assist in understanding expenditures and the ways in which they are balanced by income. These are line-item budgets, i.e., they are organized by itemizing separate costs and separate sources of income line by line.

In addition to the line-item budget, with its face sheet and detailed back-up information, there are a number of other reports for organizing budget information so that managers can analyze expenditures in relation to income. This section will deal with three of them:

- Cash Flow
- Program Budgets
- Functional Cost Analysis

Cash Flow

Cash flow analysis is the most critical planning tool for: a new children's program; one which is growing or adding different programs; or one which extends or is extended very much credit.

To understand cash flow, imagine that your children's program has balanced books, where everything looks rosy on paper, but at the same time it has no money in the bank to meet next Friday's payroll. Your balance sheet, which we will discuss later, does not give you this information. You want to know what your cash position is at any given time, and what it will be in the future. An analysis of your cash flow will give you the information you probably need.

If there were no such thing as credit, if every parent paid in cash every day and you paid every day for your staff, your food, electricity and telephone, there could not be a situation where the program's assets and liabilities were in balance, but its cash position disastrous. Yet, because of the differences in the time at which expenditures are made and income comes in, it is not at all uncommon to show a strong surplus on paper, while the program cannot pay its bills and its creditors are threatening to sue. Either money is flowing out of the organization much more rapidly than it is flowing in, or the inflow is mostly credit and the outflow is mostly cash. Ironically, this kind of disaster is more likely to strike a successful, growing program in high demand. Many a small organization has been wiped out by its own success, due to a lack of cash flow planning.

Format for Cash Flow Analysis
October, one month report

A. October Cash In
(Here you will list all the money that came in during October [early, late, or on time] and you will not list any money you are owed.)

Parent fees paid this month,
regardless if in advance or arrears _____

USDA for August _____

Other income during October _____

TOTAL CASH IN FOR OCTOBER _____

B. October Cash Out
List all variable cash expenditures (all the money you actually spent, not unpaid bills).

Heat _____

Supplies _____

Advertising _____

Transportation _____

Continue listing other variable cash outflows _____

Fixed Cash Out (an amount that you have figured out,
the same every month, that you must pay out monthly) _____

TOTAL CASH OUT _____
(all variable cash out added to fixed cash out)

C. Cash Flow
(A - B, Total Cash In minus Total Cash Out) _____
If A is less than B, the number will be a negative number
entered in parentheses or with a minus sign.

D. Cumulative Cash Flow
Add this month's cash flow to last month's cumulative cash flow. _____
In November, add your October cumulative cash flow to the
November cash flow, for the November cumulative.

Cash flow budget, cash flow report, and sources and uses report are different words for the same thing: an analysis of the way cash is flowing in your business. Cash flow tracks only actual cash transactions, including all the money an organization pays out, and all the money it collects. It ignores the complexity of who owes money to the program and what the program owes.

Reports on your assets and liabilities would be useful if you had to close your doors, but you don't want to close your doors; you want to meet your obligations and you want to survive.

When preparing a cash flow budget, list every item for which money changes hands, at the time the transaction occurs. Include, for example, the fees paid for a child in the month they are paid, not the month they are owed.

Do not include depreciation in your cash flow analysis, because depreciation is not a cash expense, but more like a deferred payment. Repayment of principal on a loan is included in a cash flow report, since it is a cash expense. Note that repayment of a loan is not included in the income and expense report, to be described in the next section. Do not list money you owe, or money that is owed you. Cash flow is about cash transactions when they happen.

An example of a monthly cash flow analysis is presented on page 76. Under "Cash In" in Section A, you will list all the money that actually came in to your program in the month that you received it, October in this case. Under "Cash Out" in Section B, you list all the money you actually spent; do not include unpaid bills. The difference between A and B is the Cash Flow. You want this number to be a positive one; i.e., you want more money flowing in than flowing out.

If you did a cash flow analysis for the previous month, add the total cash flow from last month to the cash flow for this month to get the cumulative cash flow.

There is one further analysis that is very useful to many organizations that operate close to the bottom line, and that is to identify your *Fixed Cash Out*. For cash flow purposes, "fixed" means all the expenditures you are obligated to make every month, an amount that you must pay out monthly. Directors need to etch that number on their brains. Including it in their cash flow is a good way to assure that they fully understand it.

To use this Fixed Cash Out concept in your cash flow, determine a single number that is the amount you have to pay out every month for your regular staff, probably your rent, telephone bill etc. List this one amount in the cash flow, under the category "Fixed Cash Out." List other expenditures that are not quite as fixed, as separate items. This step will enable you to review your Monthly Fixed Cash Out in relation to your Cash In and your Total Cash Flow.

The fixed cash out concept will be less helpful to you if your program operates very differently at different seasons of the year. Some child care programs, for example, have a smaller summer camp program for the three summer months. They need a different fixed cash out amount for those months.

The next example of cash flow analysis, on pages 80 and 81, shows an annual cash flow projection for a year ahead. The format is just the same as the monthly cash flow report, except that in this case the director is planning for the future rather than monitoring current cash flow; and the planning includes projecting costs for each month in the year. This cash flow projection is set up on spreadsheet software, with the formula for each calculation built into the cells.

Note the director has specified an amount of **$9,706.90**, which is the amount of cash this program **must produce every single month** to meet its necessary obligations, its *Fixed Cash Out.* On the left-hand side, three-quarters down the page, the director notes the itemized detail for arriving at a number, the fixed cash out. That number appears each month, under Fixed Cash Out, the same every month.

In September, the Director has taken in $12,117.50 and spent $9,906.90, so that her net cash flow is $2210.60. In October, she adds this net to her October net cash flow, and each month this cumulative cash flow grows larger and more positive, until January when some of it has to be spent to cover a cash flow loss. By July, the program is in the red, from a cash flow perspective.

Projecting cash flow enabled this director to predict that it might be necessary to secure a bank loan or line of credit to cover a temporary cash flow problem in February, and again in June/July. She could also examine other solutions since, in this case, she is planning ahead. She might use the projections to fundraise a *cash flow cushion* to protect the program from such problems. She might time her expenditures differently across the year.

Cash flow enables you to meet your responsibilities. You want to be able to pay your bills and your staff without borrowing from your suppliers. When you owe money you are borrowing from the people you owe, and those who owe you money are borrowing from you. Cash flow reports give you a good picture of how the money is coming in and out of your organization, a picture many programs need.

If your children's program is part of a larger organization, that larger organization may be absorbing any cash flow problems you might have in its larger budget. Without cash flow problems, you may find that another type of report, using *accrual accounting*, is more useful. Accrual will be discussed below.

Cash flow's advantage lies in the picture it paints of current financial reality. Its disadvantage is its inability to remind you of your future obligations. When your cumulative cash flow is strong and growing stronger at a given time, you will need to remember that you have a big insurance bill due in two months. The cash flow report by itself won't tell you that.

A cash flow report is incomplete without knowledge of what you owe, and what is owed you. Like all directors of children's programs, you will figure out what combination of reports will bring the information you need, when you need it, to manage your program.

Sample Annual Cash Flow Projection for Year Ahead

Community Day Care Cash Flow	Sept	Oct	Nov	Dec	Jan	Feb
Cash In						
Parent fees	5,117.50	4,094.00	3,864.00	4,629.00	3,651.50	3,542.00
Government vouchers	5,750.00	5,980.00	7,044.00	5,911.00	5,681.00	4,571.00
USDA	1,250.00	1,250.00	1,390.00	980.00	937.50	922.50
Total Cash In	12,117.50	11,324.00	12,298.00	11,520.00	10,270.00	9,035.50
Cash Out						
Heat	200.00	300.00	400.00	400.00	400.00	400.00
Supplies			1,437.24			1,437.24
Advertising		20.00		600.00		
Transportation				40.00	20.00	20.00
Ed. materials						
Staff develop.		225.00				
Insurance						
Legal, audit fees					1,000.00	
Total Variable Cash Out	200.00	545.00	1,837.24	1,040.00	1,420.00	1,857.24
Fixed Cash Out *	9,706.90	9,706.90	9,706.90	9,706.90	9,706.90	9,706.90
Interest on loans						
Total Cash Out	9,906.90	10,251.90	11,544.14	10,746.90	11,126.90	11,564.14
Net Cash Flow	2,210.60	1,072.10	753.86	773.10	(856.90)	(2,528.64)
Cumulative Cash Flow		3,282.70	4,036.56	4,809.66	3,952.76	1,424.12
* Fixed Cash Out (Monthly)						
Salaries				6,955.00		
Fringe 18%				1,251.90		
Elec.&Tel				200.00		
Food				1,300.00		
Total				9,706.90		
Cash on Hand at start mo.	800.00	3,010.60	4,082.70	4,836.56	5,609.66	4,752.76
Total Cash In	12,117.50	11,324.00	12,298.00	11,520.00	10,270.00	9,035.50
Cash Balance	12,917.50	14,334.60	16,380.70	16,356.56	15,879.66	13,788.26
Less Total Cash Out	9,906.90	10,251.90	11,544.14	10,746.90	11,126.90	11,564.14
Cash on Hand end mo.	3,010.60	4,082.70	4,836.56	5,609.66	4,752.76	2,224.12

Mar	Apr	May	June	July	Aug	Total
3,864.00	3,864.00	5,117.50	3,749.00	3,749.00	3,519.00	48,760.50
5,836.00	5,359.00	5,635.00	-	-	18,935.00	70,702.00
882.50	885.00	1,012.00	855.00	825.00	900.00	12,089.50
10,582.50	10,108.00	11,764.50	4,604.00	4,574.00	23,354.00	131,552.00
400.00	300.00	200.00				3,000.00
		1,437.24			1,437.24	5,748.96
			800.00		600.00	2,020.00
		20.00	20.00	30.00	30.00	180.00
					300.00	300.00
225.00					50.00	500.00
					400.00	400.00
						1,000.00
625.00	300.00	1,657.24	820.00	30.00	2,817.24	13,148.96
9,706.90	9,706.90	9,706.90	9,706.90	9,706.90	9,706.90	116,482.80
10,331.90	10,006.90	11,364.14	10,526.90	9,736.90	12,524.14	129,631.76
250.60	101.10	400.36	(5,922.90)	(5,162.90)	10,829.86	1,920.24
1,674.72	1,775.82	2,176.18	(3,746.72)	(8,909.62)	1,920.24	
2,224.12	2,474.72	2,575.82	2,976.18	(2,946.72)	(8,109.62)	
10,582.50	10,108.00	11,764.50	4,604.00	4,574.00	23,354.00	
12,806.62	12,582.72	14,340.32	7,580.18	1,627.28	15,244.38	
10,331.90	10,006.90	11,364.14	10,526.90	9,736.90	12,524.14	
2,474.72	2,575.82	2,976.18	(2,946.72)	(8,109.62)	2,720.24	

Spreading Cost Allocations

Several tools for managing money call for thinking about your spending in categories of costs. *Program budgeting,* for example, helps you to figure out what you are spending on each of the programs you run. *Functional cost analysis,* for another example, helps you to know what you are spending on particular functions, or categories of costs.

The Program Budget

If you run a single child care center or nursery school, your line-item budget is a *program budget* because you are running one program. If, on the other hand, your preschool program is a part of an elementary school system, its line items may be incorporated into an overall budget for the whole system, making it difficult for anyone reading the budget to figure out what the preschool program really costs. Even in a single-site children's center, you may decide to add a new center in another location, or add a family child care satellite system, or an infant care service, or evening hours. You will understand better what is happening if you keep your numbers separated on paper, considering them as "programs" for financial purposes.

Program budgeting enables you to understand and evaluate costs and income program by program. For example, you might find that your evening hours program, which you have been considering dropping, is actually paying the fixed costs for your infant program. That is useful information. Of course, you will continue to view your entire program as a whole for other management purposes.

To create a program budget, organize your costs and income by program, in the following steps. Start with your annual line-item budget. Set up your columns with the line items on the left. The sample program budget, on page 83, is from a child development center that offers a preschool program, an infant/toddler one, and a network of family child care homes.

1. Most of the costs of each "program," such as the salaries of staff who work only in one "program," will clearly belong in the budget of the identified "program." There will be a few central costs that are shared across these "programs." For example, there might be a social worker working 50% of the time in each of two "programs." The director is

This is a Sample Program Budget

LINE ITEM	PRESCHOOL PROGRAM	FAMILY CHILD CARE	INFANT PROGRAM
Director			
Administrative staff			
Classroom staff			
Maintenance/domestic			
Health/social service			
Cook			
Other personnel			
Fringe benefits			
Consultants, contract services			
Supplies			
Occupancy			
Vehicle & equipment			
Conferences, events			
TOTALS			

Worksheet #1

This is a **Worksheet Format for Calculating Payroll Costs in Functional Cost Analysis**

July 1, _____ – June 30, _____

Oldtown Children's Center

Gross Pay Plus Employer's Share of Benefits
(Some figures inserted as examples)

NAME & POSITION	GROSS PAY & FRINGE	ADMINISTRATION	FEEDING	CARE AND TEACHING	HEALTH SERVICES	TRANSPORTATION	OCCUPANCY	PARENT SERVICES	SPECIAL FUNCTIONS
J. Birdfoot *Director*	$24,375	$20,900						$ 495	$2,980
B. Fairchild *Cook*	$ 9,000		$9,000						
M. Kosia *Social Worker*	$11,050							$11,050	
A. Frendly *Classroom Teacher*	$16,000			$16,000					
D. Peng *Driver, Maintenance*	$ 9,090					$4,545	$4,545		
continue whole payroll									

→

the director of each of the "programs," and the cost might be allocated equally across them, or it might be allocated by an estimate of the amount or percent of time the director spends on each "program" and a column for each program you want to identify.

2. Spread each expense item across the programs.

3. Do the same thing for income items.

Your format might look like the one on page 83.

Functional Cost Analysis

Functional cost analysis can be used as a form for your budgeting if you find it provides helpful information. It becomes helpful when it is important to compare the costs of different "programs." Spreading your budget into functional categories seems a lot like program budgeting, but it is done differently and for a different purpose. It is a subset under program budgeting. The purpose is to enable you to compare costs by function.

When public funds are involved, as in setting rates for government reimbursement for subsidized children, cost analysis makes cost comparison possible. Some states have used cost analysis to predict the effects of a change in licensing rules.

You will notice in an earlier section on rules of thumb, there is historic cost data from twenty centers. Using a standard functional budget system, policymakers are able to compare accurately the costs of different programs by comparing what they spend on certain functions.

A program, for this purpose, means any parts of your operation that have different costs and provide different services. Of course, to you it remains an integrated, single program, but separating out the costs can provide you with useful information. If you manage several programs, functional cost data permit you to compare the costs of your different functions to see whether they reflect your priorities for how you want to spend your dollars. You might find that one program has higher administrative costs than you want, or that transportation costs more, in relation to the overall budget, than is feasible. You might try to develop programs that have the potential to help you pay for some of your other programs. Functional analysis can help you understand your own costs. It can help funding sources decide what to pay you, by comparing your costs with those for the same functions in other programs.

> **The eight standard functions that are usually used for cost analysis in children's programs are:**
>
> - Care and Teaching
> - Administration
> - Feeding
> - Health Services
> - Transportation
> - Occupancy
> - Training and Special Events
> - Parent Services

These eight functions are not the same as the items in the line-item budget at the beginning of this book. You will note that there is no line item for supplies, for example, since supplies are used within the different functions of the children's program. Some are used for care and teaching, some for administration, some occupancy, some for feeding, and some for health. There is no personnel section, since the people costs will be attributed to the functions they perform.

Some staff salaries will be budgeted entirely in one function, such as those of classroom teachers who perform no other functions. Some will be spread over several functions, such as the salary of a social worker who also does the bookkeeping. In preparing a functional budget, it is not useful to nit-pick over minor matters, such as adding up, under the occupancy function, ten minutes of watering plants or dusting the windowsill done by a director or a classroom teacher. Keep it simple.

The function of feeding includes all the costs for food, paper cups, and other supplies, plus the time spent by the cook preparing the food. The items for payroll, supplies, and equipment will have to be spread across the different functions. In the case of supplies, the program's bookkeeping system needs a Chart of Accounts that differentiates items of supplies and equipment by function. Functional cost analysis for supplies is easier to do if the chart of accounts matches the functional categories for supplies. Supplies and equipment then would be entered into the program's ledger with numbers that relate to their function, so that costs by function can later be compiled. In the example, Worksheet #1, the program does not record supply expenditure by function, and therefore is using a spreadsheet to spread these costs appropriately by function.

Payroll analysis is done either by research that requires each staff person who might perform more than one function to fill out time sheets for a designated period, or it is estimated by percentages based on knowledge of how staff spend their time. The first method results in a lot more information, because no one can know accurately how staff spend their time without some research. However, time tracking is burdensome for staff, and a director may have reasons to postpone it. At some point it is a good idea for any program to make the effort to track how its paid time is spent. Meanwhile, directors can initially proceed with a less accurate estimate in the interest of harmony.

To analyze costs by function, the director uses four worksheets as steps. Worksheet #1 is on page 84 of this section. Worksheets #2, #3 and #4 are on pages 88, 89 and 90 of this section.

1. Worksheet #1: Breakdown of how staff costs are used; shows you how to assign money for staff to the correct column of functions spread out horizontally on a page.

2. Worksheet #2: The same analysis for supplies, spreading the cost of different types of supplies horizontally across the appropriate functional column.

3. Worksheet #3: With the data from these two worksheets, the director can spread all the costs of each program across the functional areas, working from the budget.

4. Worksheet #4: The final step is to take the functional totals and set their names on the left-hand side of the page as if they are line items.

This is a Worksheet Format for Calculating Supplies Costs for Functional Cost Analysis

July 1, _____ – June 30, _____

Oldtown Children's Center

JULY	SUPPLY ITEMS	ADMINISTRATION	FEEDING	CARE AND TEACHING	HEALTH SERVICES	TRANSPORTATION	OCCUPANCY	PARENT SERVICES	SPECIAL FUNCTIONS
1	Best Foods		$500						
3	Smilio Toys			$175					
3	Diapers			$ 45					
5	Envelopes	$30							
7	Gasoline					$35			
8	Rental Film								$50
8	Conference Refreshments								$40
9	Paper Cups		$ 25						
11	Oil						$400		
14	Floor Cleaner						$ 20		
16	Art Supplies			$100					
	TOTALS	$30	$525	$320		$35	$420		$90

Worksheet #3

Functional Cost Analysis for a Single Program

Transform **all** line items into functional categories.

LINE ITEMS	ADMINISTRATION	FEEDING	CARE & TEACHING	HEALTH SERVICES	TRANSPORTATION	OCCUPANCY	PARENT SERVICES	TRAINING & EVENTS	TOTAL $ OR PERSON HOURS
List staff totals Worksheet #1									
List supplies totals Worksheet #2									
List all other line items and spread									

Worksheet #4

Functional Cost Analysis for a Single Program

Final Step: List Costs by Function.

FUNCTION	PERSONNEL COSTS BY FUNCTION	NON-PERSONNEL COSTS BY FUNCTION	TOTAL COSTS BY FUNCTION	PERCENT OF TOTAL
Administration	$ _____	$ _____	$ _____	_____ %
Feeding	$ _____	$ _____	$ _____	_____ %
Care and Teaching	$ _____	$ _____	$ _____	_____ %
Health Services	$ _____	$ _____	$ _____	_____ %
Transportation	$ _____	$ _____	$ _____	_____ %
Occupancy	$ _____	$ _____	$ _____	_____ %
Parent Services	$ _____	$ _____	$ _____	_____ %
Staff Training and Events	$ _____	$ _____	$ _____	_____ %

5 Budget Reports

This section will describe three other budget tools that directors find useful for managing the finances of their programs. They are:

- Deviation Reports
- Balance Sheets
- Accrual Budget Reports and Income Statements

Deviation Reports

A budget has little value unless the director of the program continually seeks and receives information about what is currently happening with the money, and can act on that current information. A number of different kinds of reports that summarize financial activity can be prepared. Often survival, and always quality, depend on them.

Using the familiar format for income and expenditures, a *deviation report* compiles information on what has been spent to date, or in a particular month, compared with what was planned in the budget. At least quarterly, it is important for a program to compare actual spending with planned spending, and to identify any deviations from the plan. Sometimes the deviations you find make sense because you planned to make the expenses and knew where to find the income to cover them. Those that come as a complete surprise are the ones that should concern you as the director. You need to detect deviations before they turn into cumulative disaster.

You can also report deviations in a cash flow format, or even in a functional budget format. You should do it, or get your accountant to do it, in the form that is most useful to you in making the kind of decisions you need to make.

The examples that follow combine an income/expense budget with deviation analysis as a management tool. One is an example of a monthly deviation report. The second is a report prepared at intervals throughout the year. In the second example, which would be prepared quarterly, the first column is the amount spent at this point in the year, "to date." The second column is the total amount you had budgeted to cover the period up to this point. The third column gives the deviation in dollars, and the last column gives the percent that the budget deviates from the planned budget for each line item.

Form for a Monthly Deviation Analysis
Income and Expenditures

Month_____ Year_____

	A	B	C	D
	ACTUAL FOR MONTH	BUDGET FOR MONTH	DEVIATION B-A	% DEVIATION $\frac{C \times 100}{B}$
Revenue				
Tuition				
Donations				
Government				
Foundation				
Other				
TOTAL REVENUES				
Expenses				
Salaries				
Fringes				
Repairs & maintenance				
Consultants				
Mortgage interest or rent				
Depreciation				
Licenses & fees				
Insurance				
Telephone				
Utilities				
Supplies				
Equipment				
Food				
Travel				
Miscellaneous				
TOTAL EXPENSES				
Net Income				
Tax expense, if any				
Net profit after taxes (if for-profit)				

Form for a Year-to-Date Deviation Analysis
Income and Expenditures

Year to Date _____

	A YEAR TO DATE	B BUDGET TO DATE	C DEVIATION B-A	D % DEVIATION $\frac{C}{B}$ X 100
Revenue				
Tuition				
Donations				
Government				
Foundation				
Other				
TOTAL REVENUES				
Expenses				
Salaries				
Fringes				
Repairs & maintenance				
Consultants				
Mortgage interest or rent				
Depreciation				
Licenses & fees				
Insurance				
Telephone				
Utilities				
Supplies				
Equipment				
Food				
Travel				
Miscellaneous				
TOTAL EXPENSES				
Net Income				
Tax expense, if any				
Net profit after taxes (if for-profit)				

Balance Sheets

Balance sheets are designed to show how an organization's assets and liabilities balance out to show its net worth at a given point in time. A standard form is used so comparisons can be made. It does not present a moving picture of the financial activities of the organization, as does a cash flow report. Instead, it is like a still photograph of the organization, capturing its financial picture for a given period of time. An example follows this section.

Someone else, probably an accountant, will likely prepare your balance sheet for you. You will need to understand how to read it, and how to help others understand its meaning. To understand how to read a balance sheet, you need to know a little about the standardized format. Assets are listed first, and liabilities are listed second. Each is listed in a particular order.

Assets are listed in the order of your ability to turn them into cash and the time it would take to do so. Current Assets include all the money you have, and everything that you could fairly readily turn into cash. The most easily convertible to cash, of course, is the cash you have, so cash tops the current assets list. After cash, come the Short-term Assets, which you could turn into cash without much difficulty. Short-term Assets include, in this order: Certificates of Deposit (CDs), accounts receivable, deposits you have made that you can get back, and prepaid taxes. Next to be listed are your Fixed Assets, those assets that would be harder to turn into cash; starting with equipment, furniture and fixtures, depreciation, and ending with buildings and land and the improvements you have made in them. Total Assets should equal Total Liabilities plus Net Worth.

Liabilities are listed in the order in which you must meet them. First, Current Liabilities, which include, in turn: bills you must pay in the short term, taxes due, payment of interest and principal due in the next twelve months, and then demand loans. After Current Liabilities, Fixed, or Long-term Liabilities, which include: debts you must eventually pay, including long-term loans; property improvements made by the land-lord; and all other debts.

Net Worth is the owner's contributed equity plus retained earnings (the cumulative profit, or loss, over the years).

The *Current Ratio* gives an idea of your liquidity. It is the total current assets divided by the total current liabilities. If this ratio is less than 1:1, you are illiquid. Business analysts like to see a current ratio of 2:1. However, in a not-for-profit children's program, it is no cause for alarm if the ratio is 1:1 or just a little better.

Balance Sheet

Month _____ Year _____

○ Audited   ○ Not Audited

ASSETS

Current Assets:

Cash _____

Accounts receivable _____

Utility deposits _____

Other _____

Total current assets _____

Fixed Assets:

Land _____

Building _____

Lease improvements _____

Major equipment _____

Total fixed assets _____

Minus accumulated depreciation _____

Net fixed assets _____

TOTAL ASSETS _____

LIABILITIES AND NET WORTH

Current Liabilities:

Taxes payable, federal, FICA, state _____

Health insurance, life and accident insurance _____

Retirement _____

Accounts payable _____

Total current liability _____

Long-term Liabilities:

Loans payable _____

Mortgage _____

Other _____

Total long-term liability _____

Net Worth:

Owner's contributed equity _____

Retained earnings _____

Total net worth _____

TOTAL LIABILITIES AND NET WORTH _____

Accrual Budget Reports and Income Statements

If your program is protected from cash flow problems, you might decide to develop your regular budget reports in *accrual* form. *Income statements, income/expenditure reports* and *profit and loss reports* are all the same thing, and customarily use accrual methodology. Accrual reports spread any large, uneven lumps of expenditures evenly across the months of the year. It is like putting aside part of your budget each month, on paper, to pay these known expenses. Such reports are accurate and helpful, and they enable you to avoid mistaking a temporary favorable cash position as a signal to spend, forcing you to reserve money for future obligations. When these statements are cast into the future, as predictions, they are called projections, or *pro forma* statements. The report is standardized to permit easy comparison and analysis. It should always be dated.

This income and expense statement is the familiar format for the line-item budget, usually using accrual methods. For example, the budget on page 20 is an income and expense statement. You could prepare your budget using accrual methods, or you could prepare the same budget in a cash flow form. For an accrual budget, you will list money that is owed you as income in this statement, and you will include as expenditures bills that are due but not yet paid. You place these items in the month in which they are due, rather than the month in which they are paid. Payments of interest on loans are listed as expenditures, but the repayment of the principal is not an expenditure. Instead it is listed on your balance sheet. The income and expenditures report is incomplete without this additional information from the balance sheet.

In the accrual form of budget, you spread the year's expenses as evenly as possible across the months, whether or not you have to pay large lump sums at particular times of year.

Combining Some of these Concepts

A number of different tools for analysis and management have been presented and explained in the preceding sections. As you become familiar with these tools, you will come to know which are most useful to you, given your particular situation. Work out your own format and your own timetable. You can use them as tools with which to compile the information you need to manage your program, regardless of the forms that are required of you for other purposes (such as reporting to your funding sources, or to the Internal Revenue Service).

A computer is a valuable time-saver once you have invested the time it takes to learn to use it. You can get generic spreadsheet and other software that will enable you to put any of the reports described above on a computer. Before investing in children's program-specific software, be sure you know what reports you will want and that the software will give you the freedom to create reports that you yourself decide you want to use, rather than limit you to what the program provides.

The forms that follow this section are examples of management tools developed in practice by directors.

Example A

Annual Budget Report and Projection

The first, a common form used by the director of a very small program for school age children, reports (in two columns for easy comparison) income and expenses for the past year, and a projected plan for the year to come. Speaking in the language of numbers rather than words, the figures explain why a fee increase has been made for the year ahead.

Example B

Director's Monthly Financial Statement

The second form is a monthly analysis of expenditures and income on which one director likes to spend two hours a month. Her first three columns are similar to a cash flow budget, with deviation analysis. This tells the director where she stands with the program's finances that month. She may find she has a lot of money in one line item, or has overspent in another. She may already know much of this information, because she made the spending decisions in the light of her budget. But the director likes to have a little more specific and timely information about these deviations, and to be sure there are no surprises.

Column 4 records what is owed to the center, and what the center owes, which helps the director understand why there is or is not cash in a particular budget item. This form therefore adds to the explanation of the finances by including analysis of credit to the cash flow information. The rest of the columns compare this month's income and expenses with the budget for the year.

Example C
Director's Quarterly Report
The third form is another director's quarterly report. His is a program budget organized by function, with a deviation analysis. This director, who operates a children's care and education program for preschoolers, a satellite family child care system, and a school-age child care program, finds it useful to compare expenditures by function and across programs.

Example A

Annual Budget Report and Projection for Next Year
Fairchild Children's Center • 1999 – 2000 Proposed Budget

59 children 18 months - 10 years 7:00 a.m. - 6:00 p.m.	ACTUAL LAST YEAR 1998	BUDGET THIS YEAR 1999	PROPOSED NEXT YEAR 2000
REVENUES AND SUPPORT			
Contributions	$ 11,951	$ 9,114	$ 15,000
Special events: net proceeds	5,025	3,000	6,000
Bequests	–	–	–
United Way allocation/request	80,500	36,200	81,000
Fees, grants, and contracts, govt.	56,032	49,750	60,000
Program Income	250,212	200,000	250,036
Sales, goods and services	–	–	–
Investment Income	2,650	1,000	3,000
TOTAL REVENUES & SUPPORT	**$406,370**	**$299,064**	**$415,036**
EXPENDITURES			
Salaries	$264,610	$175,000	$295,000
Employee health and retirement	3,600	2,700	5,000
FICA	25,000	14,600	25,000
Prof. fees & consultants	4,350	3,200	4,500
Supplies	40,000	18,000	25,000
Telephone	1,039	650	800
Postage & shipping	927	600	750
Occupancy	45,027	38,000	46,000
Equipment rental & maintenance	590	450	800
Printing, outside	–	300	500
Advertising	4,900	500	750
Transportation, local	1,233	1,500	2,000
Conferences	750	1,000	1,000
Org. dues, subscriptions	350	150	350
Replacement equipment	3,500	–	3,500
Miscellaneous	4,202	1,512	4,000
TOTAL EXPENDITURES	**$400,078**	**$258,162**	**$414,950**

Example B

Director's Monthly Financial Statement

One director's monthly analysis, combining cash flow with credit analysis (column 4) and comparing income and expense with budget.

Month of: _____

	1 MONTHLY ACTUAL	2 MONTHLY PROJECTED	3 ACTUAL VS. PROJECTED	4 PAYABLES & RECEIVABLES
INCOME				
Private income				
Welfare contract				
Government food subsidy				
Private employers				
TOTAL INCOME				
EXPENSES				
Salaries				
Subsidies				
Work-study				
Professional fees (audit)				
Supplies				
Classrooms				
Office				
Postage, copier				
Telephone				
Occupancy				
Rent				
Insurance				
Utilities				
Maintenance				
Food, consumables				
Unclassified				
TOTAL EXPENSES				

BUDGET NOTES: _____

_____

_____

5	6	7	8	9	10
YEAR TO DATE ACTUAL	YEAR TO DATE PROJECTED	DIFFERENCE OF 5 & 6	ACTUAL YTD + 4	TOTAL YTD PROJECTED	DIFFERENCE OF 6 & 8

Example C

Director's Quarterly Report — Third Quarter Budget Analysis

		CENTER PROGRAM		
		9 MONTHS	PER CENT	BUDGETED
210	Head teacher	$35,720.00	76.00%	$ 47,000.00
211	Assistant teacher	25,125.00	67.00%	37,500.00
212	Teacher aide	18,630.00	82.80%	22,500.00
213	Substitute	1,097.00	109.70%	1,000.00
230	Fringe	7,866.00	87.40%	9,000.00
240	Education consumables	2,197.80	81.40%	2,700.00
250	Education equipment	532.98	42.30%	1,260.00
260	Recreation	19.25	35.00%	55.00
200	**CARE & TEACHING TOTAL**	**$91,188.03**	**75.00%**	**$121,015.00**
310	Executive director	$ 7,759.50	73.90%	$ 10,500.00
311	Bookkeeper	3,695.00	73.90%	5,000.00
312	Receptionist/secretary	2,880.40	75.80%	3,800.00
313	Administrative coordinator	4,881.25	78.10%	6,250.00
314	Program coordinator			
315	Assistant coordinator			
330	Fringe	1,620.00	81.00%	2,000.00
340	Office consumables	784.90	83.50%	940.00
350	Office equipment	(119.64)	00.00%	190.00
360	Telephone	775.32	72.80%	1,065.00
370	Insurance	557.40	92.90%	600.00
380	Public information	85.41	89.90%	95.00
390	Miscellaneous (includes audits)	167.83	106.90%	157.00
300	**ADMINISTRATION TOTAL**	**$23,087.37**	**75.00%**	**$ 30,597.00**
410	Nutritionist	$ 3,893.40	72.10%	$ 5,400.00
411	Cooks	5,973.95	73.30%	8,150.00
412	Cooks' aides	3,523.00	108.40%	3,250.00
430	Nutritionist fringe	174.31	52.03%	335.00
431	Other fringe	825.93	48.30%	1,710.00
440	Food costs	11, 010.30	74.90%	14,700.00
441	Non-food consumables	491.68	43.90%	1,120.00
450	Kitchen equipment	00.00	00.00%	420.00
400	**NUTRITION TOTAL**	**$25,892.57**	**74.00%**	**$ 35,085.00**

FAMILY CHILD CARE			SCHOOL-AGE			TOTAL BUDGET
9 MONTHS	PER CENT	BUDGETED	9 MONTHS	PER CENT	BUDGETED	
93,380.00	81.00%	$115,000.00	$ 2,643.00	75.00%	$ 3,500.00	$165,500.00
			4,687.00	74.00%	6,300.00	43,800.00
						22,500.00
			3,858.00	184.00%	2,100.00	3,100.00
5,776.00	72.00%	8,000.00	691.00	83.00%	833.00	17,833.00
246.00	35.00%	700.00	239.00	34.00%	700.00	4,100.00
53.00	7.00%	700.00	00.00	00.00%	700.00	2,660.00
			54.00	19.00%	280.00	335.00
99,455.00	80.00%	$124,400.00	$12,172.00	84.00%	$14,413.00	$259,828.00
7,885.00	75.00%	10,500.00	3,004.00	75.00%	4,000.00	25,000.00
3,755.00	75.00%	5,000.00	1,502.00	75.00%	2,000.00	12,000.00
2,929.00	77.00%	3,800.00	770.00	77.00%	1,000.00	8,600.00
4,963.00	79.00%	6,250.00	1,272.00	79.00%	1,600.00	14,100.00
10,620.00	70.00%	15,000.00	2,646.00	76.00%	3,500.00	18,500.00
8,487.00	94.00%	9,000.00				9,000.00
3,276.00	91.00%	3,600.00	804.00	100.00%	800.00	6,400.00
1,061.00	122.00%	870.00	199.00	87.00%	230.00	2,040.00
00.00	00.00%	185.00	00.00	00.00%	50.00	425.00
803.00	77.00%	1,050.00	222.00	85.00%	260.00	2,375.00
548.00	95.00%	580.00	137.00	94.00%	145.00	1,325.00
86.00	91.00%	95.00	21.00	85.00%	25.00	215.00
234.00	109.00%	215.00	59.00	108.00%	55.00	427.00
44,647.00	79.00%	$ 56,145.00	$10,636.00	78.00%	$13,665.00	$100,407.00
4,055.00	75.00%	5,400.00	1,796.00	90.00%	2,000.00	12,800.00
						8,150.00
						3,250.00
225.00	67.00%	335.00	121.00	81.00%	150.00	820.00
						1,710.00
10,215.00	68.00%	15,000.00	609.00	36.00%	1,680.00	31,380.00
10.00		00.00	2.00	1.00%	210.00	1,330.00
						420.00
14,505.00	70.00%	$ 20,735.00	$ 2,528.00	63.00%	$ 4,040.00	$ 59,860.00

Example C

Director's Quarterly Report — Third Quarter Budget Analysis
Continued

		CENTER PROGRAM		
		9 MONTHS	PER CENT	BUDGETED
510	Floor maintenance	$ 4,188.00	52.00%	$ 8,100.00
530	Fringe	243.00		00.00
540	Occupancy consumables	1,572.00	126.00%	1,246.00
550	Occupancy repairs	594.00	10.00%	6,250.00
560	Utilities	5,544.00	77.00%	7,200.00
570	Rent			
500	**OCCUPANCY TOTAL**	**$ 12,141.00**	**53.00%**	**$ 22,796.00**
610	Mental health	$ 637.00	91.00%	$ 700.00
630	Medical contract	00.00	00.00%	420.00
640	First aid/health	143.00	82.00%	175.00
600	**HEALTH TOTAL**	**$ 780.00**	**60.00%**	**$ 1,295.00**
710	Training	643.00	92.00%	700.00
740	Training supplies	15.00	11.00%	140.00
700	**TRAINING TOTAL**	**$ 658.00**	**78.00%**	**$ 840.00**
810	Children's transportation	15,205.00	75.00%	20,300.00
840	Staff transportation	260.00	37.00%	700.00
800	**TRANSPORTATION TOTAL**	**$ 15,465.00**	**74.00%**	**$ 21,000.00**
910	Social service	3,870.00	69.00%	5,600.00
930	Fringe	250.00	63.00%	400.00
900	**SOCIAL SERVICE TOTAL**	**$ 4,120.00**	**69.00%**	**$ 6,000.00**
	TOTALS	**$173,331.97**	**73.00%**	**$238,628.00**

FAMILY CHILD CARE			SCHOOL-AGE			TOTAL BUDGET
9 MONTHS	PER CENT	BUDGETED	9 MONTHS	PER CENT	BUDGETED	
420.00	53.00%	$ 800.00	$ 117.00	59.00%	$ 200.00	$ 9,100.00
			7.00			00.00
158.00	126.00%	125.00	147.00	420.00%	35.00	1,406.00
59.00	10.00%	620.00	350.00	227.00%	155.00	7,025.00
550.00	77.00%	715.00	139.00	77.00%	180.00	8,095.00
			1,121.00	67.00%	1,680.00	1,680.00
1,187.00	53.00%	$ 2,260.00	$ 1,881.00	83.00%	$ 2,250.00	$ 27,306.00
			35.00	13.00%	280.00	980.00
00.00	00.00%	280.00				700.00
00.00	00.00%	280.00	5.00	3.00%	140.00	595.00
00.00	00.00%	$ 560.00	$ 40.00	9.00%	$ 420.00	$ 2,275.00
			938.00	223.00%	420.00	1,120.00
5.00	1.00%	350.00		00.00%	70.00	560.00
5.00	1.00%	$ 350.00	$ 938.00	191.00%	$ 490.00	$ 1,680.00
			812.00	73.00%	1,120.00	21,420.00
528.00	63.00%	840.00				1,540.00
528.00	63.00%	$ 840.00	$ 812.00	73.00%	$ 1,120.00	$ 22,960.00
3,937.00	70.00%	5,600.00	1,265.00	70.00%	1,800.00	13,000.00
246.00	62.00%	400.00	123.00	68.00%	180.00	980.00
4,183.00	70.00%	$ 6,000.00	$ 1,388.00	70.00%	$ 1,980.00	$ 13,980.00
164,510.00	78.00%	$211,290.00	$30,395.00	79.00%	$38,378.00	$ 488,296.00

7 Monitoring Expenditures and Income

The budget tools presented in this handbook have been selected because they are useful as management tools. They let you know when expenditures begin to exceed income. But a director must know more than how to assemble and understand a budget. The director must know how to use this information, and use it quickly when action must be taken.

A board needs an executive who will inform them and persuade them to act rapidly when information about the finances at the children's program is negative. Attendance records, fee collection records, cash flow projections, break-even analysis, and the other forms described in this handbook are all ways of compiling and producing information which sometimes requires action by a board, an owner, or a director. If one side of a budget changes, the other side must be changed to match, or action must be taken to correct the initial change. The action often needs to be immediate. Facing facts before they engulf you is essential to management.

Many organizations fail to act on early symptoms of financial trouble when doing so would enable them to correct the problem easily. With every week that goes by, the problem becomes cumulatively more serious. Finally, when there is no way to avoid the problem any longer, the indebtedness is so serious that it is very difficult to solve. Children's programs often have so little cash that they can seldom afford to wait for a small problem to become a crisis.

The most important day-to-day expenditure control is the *double-entry bookkeeping system,* which provides the information about how the money is being spent and how it is coming in. All children's programs need such accounting. This handbook does not include how-to information on double-entry bookkeeping. Instead, it assumes that the program will employ a bookkeeper, an accountant, or an accountant service. The accounting system provides accurate information about past income and expenses, and current income and expenses. The director will need this information, but does not necessarily need to become expert on double-entry bookkeeping.

Excellent material on accounting, budgeting, proposal writing, public relations, grants, and public funding is available from the Grantsmanship Center, 1015 West Olympic Boulevard, Los Angeles, California 90015.

These materials, developed for non-profits, are very valuable for for-profit organizations as well.

In addition, there are a number of tried and true, practical steps which a small organization *can* institute, and which a large organization *must* institute, to minimize the risk of misuse of funds, embezzlement, or theft. Being lax with procedures provides employees with temptations that could destroy their lives. The director's role is to be sure appropriate policies are adopted and implemented by staff. One expert, Malvern Gross, outlines twelve controls that should be adopted as a matter of policy. His recommendations are found below.

Internal Controls to Protect the Center's Money

1. Use pre-numbered receipts for all fees and other cash income.

2. Collection of cash should be under the control of two people when possible.

3. If you expect to receive checks in the mail, two people should open the mail.

4. All income should be deposited at once in the bank, and none of it should ever be used to pay bills or make purchases. Effort should be made to encourage parents to pay on the same day when they pay cash.

5. All disbursements, except petty cash, should be made by check, and no check should be written by the bookkeeper unless supporting documentation or approval is provided.

6. If the check signer is also the bookkeeper, two signatures should be required on all checks.

7. A person other than the bookkeeper should receive and reconcile bank statements.

8. Someone other than the bookkeeper should be the one to authorize writing-off of accounts receivable and other assets.

9. Marketable securities should be kept in the bank.

10. Records of assets should be kept, and inventories made, periodically.

11. Excess cash should be maintained in a separate bank account requiring two signatures.

12. Fidelity insurance should be carried.

(Malvern Gross)

Meeting Tax and Other Government Obligations

Not-for-profit organizations may be exempt from federal and state income taxes, gasoline taxes, property taxes and sales taxes. The tax exemption is not automatic. An organization must be incorporated as a not-for-profit corporation under the laws of a state, and must have applied for, and received, a tax-exempt number. Organizations that are not tax-exempt include private individuals, proprietary (owner-operated) agencies, and for-profit corporations.

Collecting the Rules and Other Information

Organizations operating children's programs are required to file the following forms for the federal government, as applicable:

- IRS, Form 1023 or 1024, for tax exemption as a 501(c)3 or a 501(c)4 corporation

- IRS, Form SS-4 Employer Identification Number for a tax exempt organization

- US Postal Office, application for bulk mailing postal permit

- US Department of Labor, "Significant Provisions of State Unemployment Insurance Law," prepared by Employment and Training Administration, Unemployment Insurance Service, probably also available from State Employment Security Agency

- Local District Office of the IRS, procedures and forms for the Federal Insurance Contributions Act (FICA tax)

- IRS, Form W-4 federal withholding tax certificates for employees

- IRS, Form 941, the employee withholding tax return, which must be filed *quarterly*

- IRS, Form 990, annual federal tax return for tax exempt organizations

- IRS, Form 1040 Schedule C, tax return for children's programs not tax exempt

- IRS, Forms 1096 and 1099, if you paid more than $600 to a consultant

See federal publications that can be helpful in filing these forms:

- Publication #557 - How to Apply for an Exemption
- Publication #15 - Employer's Tax Guide Circular E
- Publication #393 - Federal Employment Tax Forms

From the state government, you will need the following forms:

- Application for a state child care license, if applicable, and the licensing requirements
- Forms for Workers' Compensation and state unemployment insurance from State Employment Security Office
- Forms for annual report for incorporated organizations
- Forms for reporting child abuse at Child Protection Unit, in the state's Welfare Department or other Social Service Agency

In addition, you will want the forms for applying for funds, such as Child Care and Development Block Grant, or Temporary Aid to Needy Families, or for serving children with special needs with Department of Education funding. Obtain the forms from the state agency administering the money or the Head Start Bureau of the federal government, based in ten regional offices.

It is a good idea to file copies of all these forms (along with relevant codes and laws) in a notebook, which you keep up-to-date.

The chart on pages 110 and 111 examines the similarities and differences between for-profit and not-for-profit organizations.

Differences Between For-Profit and Not-for-Profit Children's Programs

ORGANIZATIONS ARE SIMILAR IN MANY WAYS

FOR-PROFIT	NOT-FOR-PROFIT
May take-in less money than it spends	Same
May take-in more money than it spends	Same
Must pay close attention to the bottom line	Same
Must operate in a competent businesslike manner to survive	Same
Is committed to a central mission	Same
Is private, with a public purpose	Same
Could exploit children for money	Same
Is regulated to reduce risks to children	Same

START-UP CAPITAL AND OTHER BORROWING

Can get small business loans, economic development dollars, investment, venture capital, or other equity	Has difficulty finding start-up dollars; can borrow from banks if has collateral, or from personal friends, relatives
Can borrow on credit cards	Can borrow on credit cards
Has difficulty getting gifts from individuals, foundations, United Way, etc. because not tax-exempt	Easily has access to charitable gifts if granted tax exemption
Securities laws permit a variety of equity instruments to raise capital	Cannot issue equity and debt instruments to raise capital

TAX STATUS AND ASSETS

Assets subject to public trust Dissolution may distribute to principals and investors	Assets subject to public trust Upon dissolution, must give to another not-for-profit organization
Pays taxes, claims deductions	Eligible to apply for tax exemption If granted, is exempt from federal, state, and local income tax on proceeds of exempt activities, and most investments; FUTA; state franchise tax; often sales, use, gasoline and property tax; may receive reduced bulk postal rates

OPERATING FUNDS

Not eligible for some government funds for children's services	Usually eligible for government funds
May return income to the organization for improvement and expansion, save or invest	Must return income to the organization for improvement and expansion; save or invest
May distribute profits to investors as return on investment	May not distribute profits to investors; may pay interest on loans

Differences Between For-Profit and Not-for-Profit
Children's Programs continued

LIABILITY

FOR-PROFIT	NOT-FOR-PROFIT
Proprietary form of organization has greatest liability; owner's personal assets are at risk Corporation is accountable rather than individual Board members; but law is changing in direction of potential personal liability for Board members	Not-for-profit Board has traditionally had charitable immunity; degree of immunity is no longer clear

PERCEPTION BY OTHERS

May be perceived by human service field, academics, and government people as commercial, exploitative; negative perception is very strong in some communities, less so in others	Perceived generally as altruistic
Perceived by many businesses as competent, professional, businesslike	Perceived by many businesses as less competent, run by volunteers, wasteful, inefficient, not competent, not professionally businesslike
Perceived by not-for-profit sector as low quality, motivated by money rather than the interests of children	Perceived by for-profit sector as wasteful of tax dollars, concerned for own interests rather than of the interests of children

CONTROL

Proprietary form of organization offers greatest individual control For-profit corporation must have a Board of Directors, which can have a small number of members; trend is toward greater Board responsibility	Not-for-profit corporation must have a Board of Directors; trend is toward greater Board responsibility
Responsive to source of capital	Responsive to community represented by Board

EASE OF CONVERSION

Owner/directors have had difficulty converting to non-profit because their own money is tied up in the organization; can create a separate not-for profit	Easier to convert from not-for-profit to for-profit; can also set up for-profit, separate, associated organization; can also engage in a few activities producing unrelated business income

Protecting the Program Through Insurance

A children's program can suffer many potentially expensive losses through damage caused by a fire, theft, or disaster; a vehicle collision; an accident to children, parents, or staff; costs of legal defense against lawsuits, or damages awarded if the lawsuit is lost; breach of contract; or liability for torts.

In an early handbook on legal issues for children's programs, William Aikman suggested focusing on two factors when thinking through the cost and the value of insurance: the degree of potential risk and the amount of dollars of potential loss. In each case, the alternative might be to be self-insured; that is, to gamble that the risk will be small or, if the unfortunate event happens, that the financial liability is not great.

For example, if the center were uninsured against collision, an accident would probably not bankrupt the organization. On the other hand, an uninsured personal injury liability could easily bankrupt a children's program.

The most important types of insurance coverage are often required: liability insurance, vehicle insurance, Worker's Compensation, and fidelity bonding. The most important types of insurance as employee benefits are health plans, retirement plans and Social Security (FICA).

Liability insurance protects you against the consequence of "negligence." Note that if you are not negligent, you are not covered. Most liability policies cover: accidental bodily injury when the insured is negligent; accidental damage to another person's property through negligence; expenses of immediate medical relief at the time of the accident; and the cost of legal defense against suits. Although $300,000 might be considered reasonable insurance coverage, the potential financial liability could be very great, so some programs carry insurance of $1,000,000 or even more. If your program prepares food for children, make sure the food is covered by your insurance. If not, you will want additional coverage up to $300,000. Personal property of $5000 or more should be insured separately if it is not included in your liability policy.

Children's insurance covers the cost of children's medical services that result from injuries or accidents while they are in the program's care, including any field trips provided by the program. This insurance covers accidents in which there is no negligence. These injuries are not covered by liability insurance. It pays on the basis of the injury, without determining negligence or liability. This insurance is very inexpensive and is often paid for by the parents.

Vehicle insurance is required of children's programs in many states. Automobile liability insurance is a high priority. When a program permits staff to transport children in their personal cars, it is essential that the additional liability insurance be provided. For example, a program might pay the staff person to increase the coverage to a higher level on her own automobile insurance policy. Or it is possible that the center's vehicle policy or general liability policy could include a rider to cover this use.

Fire insurance is standardized throughout the United States. It covers damage and losses caused by fire and lightning. Rates are based on the construction material, nearness to fire protection services, and property value. Be sure your policy has "extended coverage options" that extend coverage to smoke damage.

Theft insurance may be covered in a combined policy that covers fire, or it may be purchased separately. In high crime areas, theft insurance may be very expensive, or even unobtainable. In such areas, Federal Crime Insurance may be available from regular insurance agencies.

Insurance for natural disasters (like tornadoes, hurricanes, and earthquakes) may be combined with theft insurance.

Fidelity bonding: Directors, bookkeepers, or treasurers are sometimes bonded to safeguard against embezzlement.

Indemnification insurance is available to protect individual board members against personal liability. Board members are not usually personally liable, but there has been a recent tendency for courts to find board members liable if they are not diligent in their responsibilities. This type of insurance is expensive. Whether or not the insurance is purchased, it is important to train board members in their responsibilities and potential liabilities.

Worker's Compensation is required in many states if a business employs ten or more employees. Whether insured or not, an employer is liable. The employer is obligated to provide employees a safe place to work; hire competent fellow employees; provide safe equipment; and warn employees of any dangers. Worker's Compensation insurance covers the employer for these liabilities. It pays medical costs and work time lost, beyond seven days, resulting from accidents or injuries at work. Because of the employer's liability, this type of insurance is a useful protection, whether or not it is required by the state.

Unemployment insurance protects workers who are laid off and cannot find work. All employees have a right to unemployment benefits. State law determines the amount of benefits received and the length of time they are paid. If a laid-off employee claims unemployment benefits, the employer who terminated the employee must pay a share of the benefits. This share will be a continuing cost to the children's program as long as the person is not re-employed. If a laid-off children's program employee finds a job in another organization that is not covered by unemployment insurance, or if the person stays in a new job only a small amount of time, the children's program will continue to be responsible for some of the former employee's unemployment insurance.

Social Security (FICA) is more of a tax than an insurance plan, though a desirable one because of its benefits to your employees. A not-for-profit organization just starting up has a choice of whether or not to participate. Once covered, the program must continue to participate. Employers contribute 7.65% of the salaries of their staff. Send for a publication describing Social Security tax, from the Social Security Administration in Washington, D.C., or the closest regional office.

Health insurance generally covers either hospital, surgical, medical, or major medical expenses. Group policies made available at the place of employment generally lower the cost of medical care to the individual and family, and are important fringe benefits. Children's programs themselves can get health insurance as part of a group plan.

Life insurance, disability insurance, dental insurance, and pension plans are forms of benefits beyond the budget capacity of many children's programs, even on a cost-sharing basis. However, these programs might, as a service to their employees, be able to make such insurance available as an option for which the employees could pay directly, as members of a group, since individuals cannot purchase group insurance. Group plans may be available through national professional organizations.

Part Two

Self-Study and Teaching Materials

This section contains a number of teaching mini-cases and examples. These materials are intended for use by college classes or by self-study groups.

Financial management skills cannot be learned by reading about them, or being told about them by experts. You can learn them only by doing. If you use these cases as self-teaching materials, try to work with at least one other person, and preferably with a small group; that way, you will have a chance to see and think about differences in the way several of you did the work. Without that reality check, you can teach yourself errors. Classes and study groups work best.

Because budget is policy, a good administrator must be involved in the development of the budget. It is critical that administrators become competent using numbers for forecasting and guiding future policy. The cases that follow provide tools for managers. They can be done either with pencil and paper, or with spreadsheet software on a computer.

Directors can choose software developed specifically for administrators of children's programs, or generic business software that you can adapt to your own purposes. Be sure your software allows you to develop the information you need to manage the future, and that it does not limit you to particular tasks. Generic business software may have the versatility you need.

Technology is the administrator's friend. Once you have learned to use a computer and a spreadsheet program, you will find that spreadsheets greatly simplify budget making and financial reporting. These computer programs are more alike than different, and are a great help in the kind of work with numbers that is inherent in doing a budget or a report.

A computer is not the only tool for working with numbers. You can still use manually prepared worksheets and spreadsheets on ledger paper. With your calculator or your adding machine, or just your pencil and paper and a good eraser, you can do all of the calculations necessary. However, when you change even one number, you need to get out your eraser to change all of the other numbers that are impacted by the one number you originally changed. And when you must reduce four line items to balance your budget, it can take a frustrating amount of time to change the addition in each and every column. A computer spreadsheet, once it has been developed/programmed, makes all of the related changes automatically when you change any number.

Give some thought, if you have not already done so, to deciding when (not whether) you will learn to use a computer spreadsheet program. If you have no computer experience, you can do the following exercises with paper and pencil. Or you can combine your learning needs, mastering both the computer and the assignment at the same time. The later, more complex case examples will be easier for you if you use a computer, even though the learning curve may frustrate you.

THE CASES AND MINI-EXAMPLES

The following is a list of the case examples:

1. Comparing Three Child Care Program Budgets

2. Steven Cuts a Budget

3. Preparing the Kiddieland Budget

4. Kiddieland Nightmare

5. Kiddieland Fantasy

6. The Riverside After-School Program

7. Lincoln Child Development Center

8a. Southside Child Care: Deviation Analysis

8b. Projecting Personnel Costs at Southside

9. Martin Luther King Child Care Center

10. Good Shepherd Child Care Center

11a. Wakefield Children's Center: Program Budget

11b. Wakefield Children's Center: Functional Cost Analysis

12. Marketing Jack and Jill

13a. Breaking Even at The Children's Place

13b. Adding a Classroom at The Children's Place

Participants in administrative seminars who shared and discussed their work in classes were the principal parties in developing these case materials. Some of the participants wrote cases, as did instructors who have taught the courses over the years. The cases have subsequently been used in other administrative seminars where the principal parties were not present.

The examples are written to conceal the identities of the individuals and programs involved and, for that reason, some details have been changed. In refining the material for broader use, efforts have been made to clarify the writing, trying to develop the focus on a particular learning issue and to limit the information on background issues. Most of them are intended as short mini-examples. There are one or two "real cases," however, where the learner has to figure out what information is necessary for decision-making without any behind-the-scenes guidance from the case writer.

Public policies continue to evolve. They vary from state to state and a current policy in one state may never have been a policy in another state. Some of these case examples refer to public policy that has now changed in administrative detail. This historical material is still useful in giving participants a feel for what it is like to deal with government. In broad outline, the center/funder relationship remains very similar.

Each case is being used as a learning experience in regard to a specific financial management topic. They are sequenced to some extent, in that the later cases build on the skills developed in those that come earlier in the list. All public policy detail should be considered as obsolete background, since it is either based on a past example, or an example that will become obsolete after the publication of the book. Some further information is included in a teaching note.

I hope that you will find these case examples interesting and challenging as you work to improve your financial management skills. I would greatly appreciate your feedback regarding your experience using these mini-examples and case material, and your contribution of new examples. I can be contacted at: Wheelock College, 200 The Riverway, Boston MA, 02215.

Brief Learning Objectives of Cases

The following are some of the learning that groups of directors and would-be directors can find in the case examples. In real life, however, there is no instructor framing the questions or limiting the responses. Administrators are responsible for the questions as well as the answers they find in this material. Try to form your own questions before you look at those suggested below.

Case No. 1. Comparing Three Child Care Program Budgets

An introduction to what a *line-item budget* looks like, what it does and doesn't tell us. What is a budget? What does it look like? What are some understandings about budgets that we all share? What can be learned about a program by a concentrated review of its budget? Can we discern some messages we didn't see at first?

Case No. 2. Steven Cuts a Budget

First practice in dealing with a budget imbalance. Can you solve the problem by paring away non-personnel costs? What can you cut that will help the situation, without undermining your program?

Case No. 3. Preparing the Kiddieland Budget

How do we get from words to numbers? What data is collected as background for budget preparation? What determines the amount you will have to spend? What documentation should be developed to support budget preparation? Can you spend more than you take in? The resulting budget is a line-item budget. You can use this example to set up your budget on a computer. By doing so, you will learn in the Nightmare and Fantasy cases how easy it is to change a budget on a computer.

Case No. 4. Kiddieland Nightmare

This is the ultimate in budget cutting. How is a budget revised when unexpected developments make changes necessary? What is a deficit? How many ways are there for dealing with a deficit? The student prepares yet another line-item budget and tries to balance it. If working with a computer, the student will learn how to make changes in a budget already prepared in the computer. Can a non-profit program be bankrupt? What alternatives does this program have?

Case No. 5. Kiddieland Fantasy

How creative could we be if there were no limitations on our budget? How can we break free of self-imposed constraints? What means of discussion would work best in the "fantasy" situation? Fantasy requires the student to produce another line-item budget, or to make changes in a Kiddieland budget that you have already set up on a computer.

Case No. 6. The Riverside After-School Program

How can budgets guide decision-making? Do you ever need to project budgets for more than one year? When a budget has been done on an electronic spreadsheet, can it be copied to a new document and edited/changed? This example enables the student to investigate the future feasibility of a program, by *comparing line-item budgets over several years.*

Case No. 7. Lincoln Child Development Center

How can budgets help with decisions, and with choosing among options? How can a director best format information when she wants to make comparisons? The example compares alternatives for financing the space. The student learns to compare line-item budgets.

Case No. 8a. Southside Child Care: Deviation Analysis

When and why is *deviation analysis* done? This case uses the budget as a financial management tool by identifying and thinking about all deviations from the planned budget. The student learns to analyze deviations. How worried should you be over each deviation?

Case No. 8b. Projecting Personnel Costs at Southside

This is a brief sub-case from **Southside,** in which the student projects staff costs over a three-year period, in order to examine the effects of salary increases.

Case No. 9. Martin Luther King Child Care Center

What circumstances may require that a *budget be prepared for a period other than a year?* How do you estimate figures for a budget time period other than a year? What budget skills are needed for dealing with government? How does a budget relate to power? This example gives the student experience in *budgeting to meet government guidelines.* Formatting is a given because of government expectations. This is a historical case for which the funding details are obsolete; but it remains good practice for future funding relationships with government, and a useful case for relating budget to quality.

Case No. 10. Good Shepherd Child Care Center

Expansion decisions require budgets. What can you learn from *projecting cash flow a year into the future?* What steps would you take in response to what you learned? Do you expand when the result will be an operating deficit? What is "unutilized capacity" and how does it impact a program budget?

Case No. 11a. Wakefield Children's Center: Program Budget

The first part of Wakefield involves creating a program budget. What circumstances may lead to the decision to have separate budgets for each program within a center, i.e., for the infant classroom, the toddler classroom, the pre-school, and the after-school classroom? How can your bookkeeping divide income and expense among "cost centers"? (This is the equivalent of having a separate set of books for each program.) What software would you use for this example?

Case No. 11b. Wakefield Children's Center: Functional Cost Analysis

The third part of the assignment can be separated from the first two parts. It deals with a method for figuring out how a program's costs are distributed by functions. (See the functional budget analysis section of this book. Use the four worksheets in the book.) This assignment enables students to determine whether their assignment of funds and staff time reflects the priorities they would like to set.

Case No. 12. Marketing Jack and Jill

How does *marketing* impact on income? How does a center differentiate itself from other centers? Is accreditation valuable to centers? How do basic marketing principles impact on the utilization of children's programs? on program quality? on income? What is "unrelated business income" and what are the tax provisions that deal with it?

Case No. 13a. Breaking Even at The Children's Place

How can a break-even chart display to parents, and others, the relation between fees and income? What are the basic elements of thinking about break-even? How can a break-even chart help directors apply these concepts?

Case No. 13b. Adding A Classroom at The Children's Place

How can break-even charts help a center director understand whether it is feasible to add a new infant/toddler group? Does every classroom support its share of the center's fixed costs?

1. Comparing Three Child Care Program Budgets

In March 1995, Steven Pearlman was looking forward to his graduation from the Leadership program in the Graduate School of Wheelock College. Steven had come to the program after receiving his BS in Education from Vanderbilt University. Two years before that, he worked as a teacher in a child care program in Tennessee. He now wanted to return to Tennessee, this time as the director of a child care program.

In late March, he wrote to twenty-one children's programs in the Nashville area, finding the addresses through the state's licensing office. Of the twenty-one, he found that two were no longer in existence. He received promising replies from four centers, all of which said they expected to have turnover in the director's position within the next four months, and were willing to consider his candidacy. He decided against pursuing one of these four, because its largest component was a school-age program for children 6 - 11 years old. He wanted to work with families with younger children.

He knew that he would be happiest in a relatively small program, where he could devote his attention to his three areas of interest. They were: (1) promoting the healthy emotional and social development of young children; (2) working with the staff to foster a sense of professional development; and (3) working with parents to insure that the center's program be seen as part of a natural continuum in each child's life.

Steven wrote again to three programs that interested him most:

1. *Southside Child Center,* a program for 50 preschool children, operating five days a week, 7:45 a.m. - 5:30 p.m., 52 weeks per year.

2. *Chestnut Tree Child Development Center,* a program for 52 children, ages 2.9-5 years, operating five days a week, 7:30 a.m. - 5:00 p.m., 52 weeks per year.

3. *The Children's Place,* a program for 48 children, ages 2.9-5 years, operating five days a week, 7:45 a.m. - 5:00 p.m., 52 weeks per year.

Armed with what he had learned in his Financial Management course at Wheelock College, Steven asked each of these centers to send him a copy of its current operating budget, along with other descriptive material to help him understand the programs. Before he called to arrange for an interview at each center, Steven sat down to examine the three budgets. He wanted to see what similarities and differences existed among the three centers, to see what priorities (if any) each budget revealed, and to make up a list of questions to ask at each interview.

Exhibit 1

Southside Child Center

Operating Budget, January 1995 - June 1995

EXPENSES

Personnel		Other Than Personnel	
2 Head teachers	$ 21,000	Supplies	$ 1,024
6 Teachers	43,972	Office supplies	616
Substitutes	2,464	Equipment, child	284
2 Protective service teachers	10,000	Phone	680
Director	14,000	Audit	1,000
Bookkeeper	3,498	Insurance	3,725
Cook	3,308	Food	14,000
Substitute	352	Rent	5,300
Nurse	3,194	Maintenance	1,840
Social worker	5,600	Transportation	5,400
Fringe	16,245	Miscellaneous	500
Consultants	1,332		
Driver	5,296		
(A)	**$130,261**	**(B)**	**$ 34,369**

EXPENSE TOTAL (A + B) **$164,630**

INCOME

Office, Child/Family	$ 2,400
Welfare	90,104
Protective Services	46,046
County Commissioners	7,200
Food reimbursement	10,000
Private tuition	8,020
Southside Fund	1,400
INCOME TOTAL	**$165,170**

Exhibit 2

Chestnut Tree Child Development Center

Yearly Operating Budget, 1994 - 1995

EXPENSES

Teachers' salaries and benefits	$ 236,000
Supplies and equipment	19,600
Director salary and benefits	20,200
Insurance, bookkeeping and fees	6,300
Office supplies, communication & phones	4,000
Cook's salary and benefits	12,000
Food and milk	32,000
Food service supplies	14,000
Rent	48,000
Heat	2,000
Cleaning	12,000
Electricity	4,800
Teacher training	1,000
TOTAL EXPENSES	**$ 411,900**

REVENUES

Yearly operating from DPW	$ 381,900
Yearly funds from Food Program	30,000
TOTAL REVENUES	**$ 411,900**

Exhibit 3

The Children's Place
Budget for Fiscal Year July 1, 1994 - June 30, 1995

EXPENDITURES

Advertising	$ 1,200
Class consumables.	20,160
Health consumables.	2,400
Equipment:	
Classroom.	1,430
Office	360
Outdoor	720
Salaries.	224,520
Fringes (17%)	38,168
Food supplies.	1,200
Kitchen equipment	480
Substitutes	7,200
Insurance	2,500
Janitorial services	6,240
Food	23,000
Lease holder expense	810
Lease holder improvement.	620
License and Inspection	162
Office supplies & costs	540
Postage	480
Printing	360
Telephone.	1,200
Transportation, driver & van	17,280
Field trips	240
Equipment.	120
Insurance.	240
Audit	480
Miscellaneous	1,500
Work study.	3,520
Rent	15,840

TOTAL EXPENSES $372,970

INCOME

Department of Welfare	$291,000
Private tuition	22,000
SPED subsidy	4,690
Bureau of Nutrition	24,000
Scholarships	0
Kappa Fund	4,400
Fund raising	27,400

TOTAL INCOME $373,490

Comparing Three Budgets

Take a look at the three budgets to see what they might reveal to Steven Pearlman, even before he visits the three Nashville centers where he might want to become the director. Look at the budgets again. If they don't give you answers, they may give you clues. Read them over several times to see what you would find in them if you were Steven.

Remember that Steven did not have the advantage of a structured set of questions developed by someone else to help him. In real life, we have to think-up our own questions. Steven wanted to know what priorities, if any, each budget revealed. See what you can find in these budgets before reading the rest of this assignment. Make some notes. If you are doing this assignment in a group, try doing it first without reading the questions that follow. Have your group decide what questions Steven will ask in his interviews.

Refer to the following questions later: they may help you see more in the budgets once you have run out of ideas.

Are there any differences in the way the centers prioritize the needs of the children? Can Steven figure out a cost-per-child for each center? What would that tell him?

Can he tell if the centers are hiring and rewarding qualified teachers? What priority is given to classroom salaries in the total budget? Can he figure out the percent of the total budget spent on classroom teachers? Does the budget include a reasonable amount per-child for class-room supplies?

What are these centers like? Do we know anything about the children and parents who use them? Do the budgets provide any clues about their location? Are they urban or suburban? Can you tell anything by comparing the items for transportation or for rent? Is the population using the centers likely to be rich or poor? Do the budgets reflect any interest in a socioeconomic mix?

Steven was interested in promoting the healthy emotional and social development of young children. This interest appears to be family-supportive and preventive, rather than treatment-oriented, but we don't know that for sure. Will these three centers offer the same opportunity for a preventive, supportive approach? If Steven turns out to have a burning issue in children's programs as therapy, would one of these centers appeal over the others?

Is the emphasis on health or nutrition the same in all three centers?

Steven was interested in working with the day care staff to foster a sense of professional development. Can you find clues as to whether or not each of these centers provides support for training?

Steven was interested in working with parents to insure that the day care program was seen as part of a natural continuum in each child's life. Do we know whether all these centers offer the same opportunities in that regard?

How much will these centers be supportive of Steven as their director? What does the director earn? Are there clues that the center can pay that amount? Is the director's position full-time? What is the range of salaries, if known? What is the average salary for lead teachers? For other teachers? What help would Steven have in the office? Would he answer his own phone? Word-process his own letters? Do his own bookkeeping?

Do the budgets reflect a priority for cleanliness and maintenance? Did you notice any differences in this regard?

Did you notice differences because of the dates on the budgets?

Of course, there are many unknowns, and Steven will turn all his guesses into questions for further investigation when he gets to the center. We want to begin to develop informed guessing skills (essential for managers) and sensitivity to the potential meaning behind numbers on a page.

Make notes on what these budgets revealed to you. Compare your notes with others.

2. Steven Cuts a Budget

Steven liked The Children's Place, and the Board seemed to like him. They told him he was one of two candidates they were considering as their future director. They wanted him to understand what he was getting into, however, so they filled him in on some facts about their financial picture. They let him know they are asking both candidates to comment on the budget situation. Their choice of director may rest on these comments. In other words, they want Steven to tell them how he would change the budget for the coming year, 1995-1996.

For several years, the board had been relying on fundraising and scholarships to supplement the program's income. During a booming economy, their fundraising had succeeded, and they had come to count on it. However, their fundraising event for last year failed. Instead of raising $27,400 as anticipated, they lost $5000. In addition, given the depressed economy in their community, they see no possibility of any fundraising for the coming year. They made it clear to Steven that they would not hire a director who did not share this pessimistic view; they cannot afford to spend energy on fundraising in this economy.

They therefore have to amend their budget to show a deficit from this year of $32,400, and to remove a predicted income of $27,400 from fundraising. That makes the income side of the budget $59,400 less.

On the expenditure side, insurance costs have nearly doubled, and will be $4000 next year. The janitorial service they use is no longer willing to do snow plowing, and they were not satisfied with the service anyway. They have found a new maintenance service that will do snow plowing, but the new cost is going to be $10,000. The rent is going to increase to $20,000.

Steven asked for more detail on the salaries in the budget so he could more accurately project staff costs for the year ahead. He was given the following data on current salaries and told that everyone expects a 4% cost of living increase next year.

CHILDREN'S PLACE CURRENT BUDGET, PERSONNEL	
Director	$30,000
4 Teachers @ $21,000	$84,000
5 Assistants @ $16,000	$80,000
Bookkeeper/assistant, part-time	$15,520
Cook, part-time	$15,000

Assignment: As Steven, prepare a revised budget for the center.

3. Preparing the Kiddieland Budget

Kiddieland Children's Center was established in 1980 to serve families in western Massachusetts. It was licensed to serve 48 children between the ages of 2 years 9 months and 5 years. Marguerita Franklin became the second director of Kiddieland early in 1989. Her role was principally administrative; a head teacher/educational supervisor was responsible for the children's program. Mrs. Franklin spent much of her time with the parents.

The annual task of budget preparation was handled by a member of the board of directors, who established the yearly budget after consultation with Mrs. Franklin. In March 1989, that task fell to Jeff Davis, owner of a shoe store in the city. Davis, as a parent, had just been made Treasurer of Kiddieland's board.

On the evening of March 19, Mr. Davis sat down with Mrs. Franklin to elicit enough information to help him prepare a first draft of the operating budget for the year beginning July 1, 1989. This draft would be discussed at a board meeting, and voted on by the board as a whole. The essential parts of their conversation are reproduced below.

Davis: As I understand it, the largest expense is for salaries, right?

Franklin: Yes, we have six teachers who earn $8.00 an hour for a 35 hour week, and Sylvia, the educational supervisor, who gets $10.00 an hour. Sylvia works 40 hours a week.

D: And the center operates 52 weeks a year?

F: Right. Then there's my salary. I'll be making $19,000 a year, starting July 1.

D: How about fringe benefits: social security, unemployment tax, health insurance?

F: We have all of that, for all of us who are on the payroll half-time or more. We've figured fringe at 16% of salary for the last few years, so I guess we should stick to that figure. I do think we ought to cover the cook with our benefits, figured on a pro-rated basis. If we can, I'd like to cover the social worker, too.

D: Substitute teachers?

F: We've spent $2500 already this year on substitutes, but an awful lot of our staff were sick this winter. I'd guess $1500 is a reasonable figure for all of next year.

D: Any part-time help?

F: Not that we pay for. We have one student teacher each term from Clark University. And in exchange for supervising that student, we get one voucher each semester that allows someone on our staff to take a course at Clark. That's worth at least $1000 a year in terms of the tuition Clark usually charges.

D: How about rent?

F: That's going to stay the same next year: $12,000 a year. The increase is going to come in utilities. We're paying $3000 this year for utilities, but about half of that has been for oil heat. I'd guess the oil costs are going up about 30%; the rest should stay the same.

D: And maintenance for the center?

F: The same as this year. We have a contract with a firm that does it for $400 a month.

D: What does it cost to feed the kids?

F: We budgeted $12,000 for this year and we're just barely going to be able to stick to this figure. I'd estimate that next year's food bill will be 8% higher. The School Lunch money paid us $11,300 this year, and I expect they'll cover the increase. And Stanley's salary is going up, too. He's our cook. He works half-time for us and he's making $7275 a year at Kiddieland; but that's going to jump to $7750 a year on January 1.

D: What are you spending on supplies?

F: If you mean classroom supplies, (art materials, and things like that), we've budgeted $150 a month ever since I've been here. We've been able to stick to that, so I'd keep it the same, although it would be nice to be able to enrich the program a little more. Office supplies (like stationery, pencils and pens) and housekeeping supplies (like toilet paper, dishwashing liquids, paper towels, etc.) have always been lumped together. This year's figure is $1000, and that seems about right. We may spend a little bit under on some types of supplies, but if we do, we'll just spend the difference on classroom material.

D: What else? Any other administrative expenses?

F: Phone and postage are budgeted at $1800 this year. I'd raise that to $2000 to be on the safe side. And we spend $400 a year on advertising the center. That won't change. Our insurance costs have already been set at $2500 for next year.

D: Have we forgotten any category of expenses?

F: I'm not sure where you'll want to put these, but just last week we hired a social worker to start July 1 on a one-third time basis. That's figured on an annual salary of $22,400. She'll be spending some time here at the center and some time out with the kids' families. And the last thing I can think of is bus transportation for the kids when we go on trips. We take the older children to Sturbridge Village three times a year and that costs us $150 a trip. We'll continue doing that. If I commit us to a schedule with the bus company now for the next year, I'm sure I can hold the costs to the same we're paying now.

D: If that's it for expenses, let's move on to income. As I understand it, all of Kiddieland's income comes from parent fees or from state subsidy (Title XX) payments.

F: That's right. We have 39 children under our Title XX contract, which we just renegotiated last month, at a fee of $15 per child per day. Then there are 9 children whose parents pay $80 a week. Next year we plan to have 11 fee-paying children.

D: Do these fees get paid even when the children are absent?

F: Yes. The fees are on an enrollment, not attendance basis. The state won't pay us if absences get above a certain percentage. We also worry that if a child is absent for some time, it may mean the parent is about to stop sending him, so we try to pay attention to absences and make sure they aren't shifts in enrollment.

D: Should we budget for less than full enrollment?

F: I don't know. We're full, and we have a waiting list.

D: Anything else?

F: No that's all. I'm anxious to see what figures you come up with.

Assignment: Make a budget from this information. Write down your budget notes about the line items, to explain how you arrive at the figures you use whenever there is any calculation.

4. Kiddieland Nightmare

You are an outside consultant, brought in because of an emergency in the Kiddieland budget. You're looking at the Kiddieland budget that was prepared for 1989-90 by the Treasurer, Jeff Davis, and the Director, Marguerita Franklin, on March 19, 1989. It's now June 1, 1989, and there has been some very bad news. The Director has spent the withholding funds that were supposed to go to the Internal Revenue Service each quarter. The Center owes the IRS a substantial amount of money, including back withholding money and a penalty that the IRS insists you must pay. This is a serious problem, and the IRS is threatening to put the Director in jail and also to sue the members of the board in order to get its money. The IRS wants $20,000 from the center **immediately.** If you pay that before July 15, they'll set up a schedule for repayment of the balance-due over several years.

In addition, the price of oil has gone up, and you will need to budget $2400 for oil next year, which is more than Ms. Franklin had planned. It's been a year of heavy snow, and the maintenance company wants an extra $199 for snow plowing they had to do this winter. That leaves the center with a deficit for this year, and the money must be made up in the next year's budget. Mr. Davis can't help you because the Board blames him for the crime of spending the withholding money, and has fired him as Treasurer. The Director can't help you because she has resigned and left town. You, the consultant, have to figure this out for yourself.

Assignment: Prepare next year's Kiddieland budget. What is the total deficit for the year July 1 to June 30 next year? How will you cut the Kiddieland budget to pay these expenses? The budget, prior to cutting, is found on the next page, or you can use the one you prepared for Kiddieland. *Maybe you will wake up from this nightmare. But while it lasts, you need to use your skills to keep the Center alive through the crisis, and decide on next year's budget.*

Use the budget on the following page, or the one you developed for the "Preparing the Kiddieland Budget" Fantasy and Nightmare cases.

Kiddieland Budget

July 1989 - July 1990

50 children

INCOME

School Lunch Program	$ 12,960
State contract	152,100
Parent fees (11 @ $80/week x 52 weeks)	45,760

TOTAL INCOME **$210,820**

EXPENSES

Personnel

1 Director	$ 19,000
6 teachers @ $8/hr x 35 hr/wk x 52 wks	87,360
1 teacher @ $10/hr x 40 hr/wk x 52 wks	20,800
Cook	7,513
Social Worker, 1/3 time @ $22,400	7,466
Sub-Total, Personnel	142,139
Fringes @ 16%	21,547
Substitute teachers	1,500

TOTAL PERSONNEL **$165,186**

Other Than Personnel

Rent	$ 12,000
Oil Heat	1,950
Utilities	1,500
Maintenance @ $400 per month	4,800
Food	12,960
Classroom supplies	1,800
Other supplies	1,000
Phone and postage	2,000
Advertising	400
Insurance	2,500
Field trip transportation	450

TOTAL OTHER THAN PERSONNEL **$ 41,360**

TOTAL EXPENSES **$206,546**

5. Kiddieland Fantasy

You have just replaced Mrs. Franklin as the Kiddieland administrator. At the same time, an extremely wealthy donor has left Kiddieland a large amount of money. The provisions of the will are that Kiddieland should continue their program for 3-5 year old children, and should make it a high quality program that pays good salaries to its teachers. The donor set up a fund that would pay whatever Kiddieland needed to continue to charge the same fees for parents *and* be able to spend more to improve the quality of their program, especially the salaries. Each year the director of Kiddieland is to ask the trustees of the donor's estate for what funds are needed that year to balance the budget.

Assignment: As Director, you have two tasks. First, decide what the budget process should be. Who should be involved in making the budget? When you took the job, the Board told you that they were willing to have you set up a new budget process.

Second, in preparation for meeting with those who you determine are involved in the process, prepare a budget for discussion. Take Kiddieland's current budget, developed by Ms. Franklin and Mr. Davis in a previous case, and add a new line item, called Donor Fund, to the income side of the budget. Leave it blank until you revise the expenditure side.

Revise the salaries and any other items necessary to make the donor's wishes a reality. "Fair salaries" would mean upper-end of the current salaries being paid in the field. "A quality center" would mean adding whatever you thought was not adequate in the line items Mrs. Franklin discussed with Mr. Davis.

Total the expenses. Determine the amount to ask the donor's estate for the Donor Fund line item.

6. The Riverside After-School Program

The Riverside Community Center was built in a southern city in 1970 to house a variety of programs for children and adults. Among the activities located in the center were Boy Scout and Girl Scout meetings; swimming; exercise classes for children, teenagers and adults; games, snacks, and dancing for high school students; and social events for senior citizens. The Center was soundly built, was extensively renovated in 1986, and again in 1995.

In 1988, with funds from a federal program, the city of Riverside was able to build a senior citizens' complex that included housing and facilities for social and recreational activities. As a result, the senior citizens' social hall at the Community Center was no longer needed; it was only used for community events.

At their monthly meeting in November 1997, the Board of Directors of the Community Center discussed alternative ways to use this valuable community space on a more regular basis. After some discussion, one of the Board members indicated that he would be willing to contribute $15,000 to the Community Center to adapt the room as an after-school program for elementary school children. The only stipulation he placed on the gift was that the fee to parents for use of the center could not exceed $1.00 an hour for the first three years of the program's operation. The Board of Directors agreed to consider this offer, and discuss it at their December meeting.

Ms. Charlotte Webb was invited to the December meeting, as the guest of two of the Directors, to help and advise the Board about setting up a school-age program. Ms. Webb, a resident of Riverside, was employed as a co-director of a school-age program in Cooperville, a neighboring city.

At the meeting, Ms. Webb discussed with the Board some of the parameters she thought should be established to insure a successful program. She indicated that a new Riverside after-school program should accommodate a maximum of 25 children, given the space available, and that it be for a limited age range. She suggested 5 to 8 years as an appropriate age range. She believed that a staff of two experienced teachers would be the minimum necessary to provide adequate supervision and attention to the children. The director of the program could be one of the two teachers. She gave the Board a copy of the licensing regulations for the state, which are not stringent. The state permits 25 children with one group leader, but Ms. Webb recommended two adults with the children.

Part of the day, however, the Director could carry out her administrative responsibilities.

The Board of Directors continued to meet after Ms. Webb finished her presentation and left. They were all impressed by her knowledge of the topic, as well as by her seriousness and competence. They agreed to ask her to prepare a three-year budget for the proposed after-school program, with the understanding that if the program became a reality, they would like to hire her as the first teacher/director.

In a phone conversation the next day with one of the Board members, Ms. Webb indicated her interest in the proposition, and she agreed to try to spell out for the Board what costs might be incurred in years 1, 2, and 3 of such a program. She agreed to prepare the budgets in such a way that per child fees could be held to the $1.00 an hour that the donor had stipulated.

Over the following few weeks, Ms. Webb jotted down all the information she could gather on the costs of equipment, supplies and the labor necessary to adapt space for use as an after-school program. Her notes are reproduced below.

Hours of operation: 2:00 - 6:00 p.m., 5 days a week, 40 weeks a year, following the school schedule.

Staffing: One director/teacher, to be paid $12/hour. Assume she works 7:45 a.m. to 12:15 p.m., basically a four-hour day with an extra 15 minutes before and after hours to open up, clean up, and plan the program. She is paid for a workday of 4 1/2 hours/day. One associate teacher, to be paid $10/hour, also is paid to work 4 1/2 hours/day. These salaries are about 10% higher than the going rates around Riverside, but the work is part-time and there are no fringe benefits. For years 2 and 3, build in an 8% salary increase each year.

Tables and Chairs: Can buy 6 sturdy, high quality sets (table + 4 chairs), for $290 a set.

Carpentry: Have to build cabinets, bookshelves, a couple of nooks, platform along one wall, coat pegs, etc. Carpenter estimates 2 people would take 2 weeks to finish the job at $600 per person per week. Figure an additional $1400 for materials. (Note: carpenter has also offered to build and finish six tables for us, to match shelves and cabinets rather than buying table-and-chair sets. Figure this would add one more carpenter working one more week, and would raise the cost of materials to $1800. Worth it? It's cheaper to buy chairs than to have them made. Can get 24 chairs at $34 each).

Painting: After carpentry is complete, figure 2 painters working 4 days each at $20/hour (i.e., $160 a day). This figure includes paint costs.

Floor covering: $1300 quoted by local store for the entire job, including laying carpet. [They're willing to give us three-year terms. Payments would be $500, $400, and $400. (Worth it?)]

CD players/Video player: Figure one of each @ $150 each.

Books: Figure 50 at an average price of $12.

CDs: Figure $360.

Easel and paints: 5 two-sided easels at $90 each. Tempera paints at $150 for a year's worth.

Games: Plan on 20 items, at an average of $20 each.

Other supplies: $800.

TV: Rent, beg, or buy? Cost?

Balls, jump ropes, etc.: $100.

Blocks: Can get set for $750. Shelves $250.

Computers and modem: Try to get donated equipment.

Assignment:

1. From information given, prepare budgets for 1998-99, 1999-2000, and 2000-01. Assume that the program will be operating at full enrollment.

2. Follow Ms. Webb's staffing notes. For the other items, you are free to depart from Ms. Webb's plans if you have good reasons. Your ideas for the kinds of activities to offer may differ from Ms. Webb's. Write line-item notes, justifying any change you made in the items and figures mentioned by Ms. Webb. Add any comments you feel are necessary to explain your calculations.

3. Do not include on the income side of your budget a line item called "fundraising." Do not list donated items unless you can document a real place where such donations are readily available, such as a factory outlet.

4. Decide whether the two staff members would receive any pay raises during the 3-year period.

5. What do your figures tell you about the feasibility of the $1.00 fee across the 3-year period?

7. Lincoln Child Development Center

By September of 1997, Linda Cooley had made up her mind: the Center would move to a new location, and it would move as soon as possible. As Director of the Lincoln Child Development Center, she had been through too many unpleasant experiences to consider staying in the present location any longer. What she wanted to do now was sit down and figure out what kind of move made the most sense for the Center, and determine what impact a move would have on the budget and on the Center's staffing pattern. She wanted to move. Christmas, she thought, wouldn't be too soon.

Background: The Lincoln Child Development Center provided comprehensive services for 26 children between the ages of 2 1/2 and 6. The Center was open five days a week from 7:45 a.m. until 5:00 p.m. The center was located one block from downtown Lincoln, on the first two floors of a renovated, three-story brick factory building. The first-floor classroom had over 300 square feet. There was a large outdoor play yard adjacent to the Center. It was designed to allow for a wide variety of large-motor activities and experiences with sand, earth, and plants.

The City of Lincoln and its surrounding communities is an area that is mostly residential, with a few small factories and small retail stores. Most of Lincoln's employed population worked at blue-collar jobs. The Lincoln Child Development Center opened in the summer of 1976 to serve low-income families in Lincoln. The Child Development Center was one of several programs operating under the umbrella of the Lincoln Community Agency (L.C.A.). L.C.A. was funded by the federal Community Services Administration. The goal of its various programs was to help eliminate poverty in Lincoln.

Linda Cooley was hired in 1993 as the fourth director of the Lincoln Child Development Center. In an interview two years later, she described the demand for children's programs in Lincoln:

Quality child development is needed in Lincoln and the communities around it, for reasons related to employment, education, and family health. Each child currently enrolled at the Center is there for one or more of these reasons, often for all three.

In the last six months, the Child Development Center has received more than thirty requests to enroll a child. Because the Center is now operating at full enrollment, those needing immediate service have been referred elsewhere. Twenty families chose to be placed on the Center's waiting list. The two other centers in Lincoln have waiting lists of equal size.

Philosophy: The Center's philosophy was expressed in the following statement Linda prepared in 1993 for the state:

> *The Child Development Center is committed to an educational philosophy that encourages each child to emerge and grow as a unique and capable individual within an environment that is both secure and stimulating.*
>
> *The Center views learning as an integrated, ongoing experience, and thus offers a program which provides equally for the social, intellectual, physical, and affective development of each child.*
>
> *Each child at the Child Development Center is viewed as a unique person with distinct abilities and interests. The program is designed with sufficient flexibility to provide each child with a wide choice of activities. Activities are designed to give children experience and competence in many areas, including Creative Expression, Communication (including math and science), Human Social Interactions, Environmental Orientation, and Physical Coordination and Competence.*
>
> *An important aspect of the center's program is the integration of children of various abilities. In this way children learn from one another, and learn to respect their own unique abilities and limitations, and those of others, as they approach experiences.*

Outdoor play and other large-muscle activities were an important part of the Center's program. Weather permitting, children played outside for at least an hour each day. Other large motor activities were offered indoors. The upstairs classroom had one head teacher (who was certified as a teacher of children with special needs) and one assistant teacher working with ten children. Downstairs were two teachers who were co-leaders, and one part-time assistant teacher. Typically, the children were all together in one room in the early morning and late afternoon. For most of the day, the children were divided between the two classrooms.

Each team member planned and implemented activities for small groups and individuals. Planning for large group field trips and special projects was done as a team. General themes, used as a basis for activities, were decided by the individual teams. [Responsibilities of team members are detailed in Exhibit 2.] Anyone working with children on a volunteer or student teaching basis was expected to participate in planning activities and to maintain a regular schedule of attendance.

The Child Development Center maintained formal and informal working relationships with a wide variety of local agencies and organizations. Through these contacts, the Center was advised of families needing day care. In turn, these agencies provided staff at the Center with sources to which they could refer families needing services. A full-time parent coordinator worked at the Center, and was responsible for insuring an effective outreach program. She relied primarily on contacts with local agencies, in addition to newspaper publicity and word of mouth. A daily schedule at the Lincoln Child Development Center in 1996 follows.

Exhibit 1

Lincoln Child Development Center

DAILY SCHEDULE

7:45 - 9:00 a.m.: Arrival time: Open Classroom. Children choose among activities prepared as options by staff, including: science, sand and water play, art, games, and dress-up.

9:00 - 9:30 a.m.: Prime Activity time. Children work in small groups on special projects in a variety of curriculum areas.

9:30 - 9:45 a.m.: Large Group Meeting. Teachers lead large-group activities, including music, creative movement, verbal expression, physical exercises.

9:45 - 10:00 a.m.: Snack.

10:00 - 11:00 a.m.: Activity Time: Pre-reading and pre-math. Children participate in small, assigned groups in reading and math-related activities.

11:00 - 11:30 a.m.: Clean-up and Lunch. Emphasis on socialization. Lunch served in individual portions with children participating in table setting and cleaning up.

11:30 - 11:45 a.m.: Bathroom, tooth brushing.

11:45 a.m. - 12:45 p.m.: Outdoor Play (weather permitting) or indoor physical exercise.

12:45 - 1:00 p.m.: Quiet Time. Story reading, nap preparation.

1:00 - 3:00 p.m.: Nap, rest period.

3:00 - 3:15 p.m.: Wake up period, snack.

3:15 - 5:00 p.m.: Open Classroom. Children choose among activities offered by staff, including: story telling, dress-up, blocks, art, educational games, and dramatic play.

Arrivals and Departures: Because the Center was located within walking distance of most of the children's homes, and was only two blocks from a bus stop on the main Lincoln bus line, parents were responsible for transporting their own children to and from the Center each day. This arrangement helped insure daily personal contact between families and teachers. The director believed that the parents' frequent visits to the center fostered a deeper understanding of Center procedures, a friendly rapport with teachers, and a more direct involvement with program needs, problems, and events.

Financial Management: Responsibility for the financial management of the Lincoln Child Development Center was shared between Linda Cooley, the Center's director, and the Fiscal Department of L.C.A., the umbrella agency. Ms. Cooley prepared the annual operating budget for the Center, and monitored expenditures on a monthly basis. The L.C.A. financial officer maintained all financial records and was responsible for all receipts and disbursements. The L.C.A. Fiscal Department was also responsible for submitting funding reports to any funding sources, and maintaining personnel and compensation records. For these various services, L.C.A. charged the Center a flat 6% of total budgeted operating expenses as its annual fee.

The Center's operating budget for the 1996-1997 year is given in Exhibit 3. Tuition for all children enrolled at the Center was paid by the Department of Public Welfare. Twenty-six children were paid for at a rate of $23.50 per child per day, under a donated funds contract. To generate these funds, the city of Lincoln donated to the Office of Child Care Services a sum equivalent to 25% of the total amount. This matching mechanism has been in place since the center began.

The two remaining children were covered by a direct service contract from DPW, under which DPW paid all costs, with no need for matching funds. The direct service contract was negotiated at a different time from the donated funds contract, and at a different rate ($20.94 per day).

The City of Lincoln gave the center a grant of $20,000 to be used for general operating funds. This money came from a HUD Community Development Block Grant and from a Small Cities Grant. Ms. Cooley remarked on how difficult it was to get the City of Lincoln to give funds to help the center each year, be it for the direct grant to the center or for the donation to DPW for the Title XX contract generated by the donated funds as match.

"It's an incredible struggle each year," she commented, "and we can never be certain in advance that the city is, in fact, going to release the funds." She estimated that she spent the equivalent of a month each year talking to city officials and eventually shepherding the funds through the appropriate channels until a contract was signed with DPW.

The Center did occasionally receive supplemental funds from fundraising events or from foundations. Subsequent to the preparation of the FY 1997 budget, the Center received a $12,000 parent education grant. The grant would cover the 12-month period between January and December 1997. Half the grant would be used toward the parent coordinator's salary; the other half would be used for the direct costs of parent education activities. Given the amount of time and effort required, Ms. Cooley put proposal writing very low on her own list of priorities for the Center. She had no plans to pursue additional grants in the foreseeable future.

Operating Issues in 1996-1997: During 1996 and 1997, the center had a number of problems, all of which were related to the physical facility. There had been four break-ins while no one was at the center. These had resulted in general vandalism, as well as several hundred dollars' worth of stolen equipment and supplies. It was virtually impossible to secure the center against such break-ins, because the adjoining factory provided such easy access to it.

The most serious catastrophe occurred in February 1997. Late one Friday afternoon, the water pipes in the factory above froze and burst, flooding the center all weekend. This resulted in relocation for a week, providing limited care for those children in dire need. The staff members spent half days cleaning and restoring the center and half days with the children. The center eventually had to spend $1600 on repairs, for which the landlord never reimbursed them. Because nothing had been changed in the building's plumbing system, there appeared to be nothing to prevent the same situation from recurring in the coming winter.

Ms. Cooley was determined to relocate the center at the earliest possible date. During the month of May 1997, she spent 10 days investigating other possible locations for the center in Lincoln, considering both rental and purchase options. All the buildings to which she gave serious consideration were located in downtown Lincoln. By the end of June, she had narrowed her choice to four buildings: two of them rentals, and two purchases. All four buildings provided adequate indoor and outdoor space, although the costs varied widely and some of the buildings would need substantial renovations. (See Exhibit 4 for information on the four buildings.)

Ms. Cooley realized that there was no surplus in her 1996-1997 operating budget to use toward the purchase, rental, or renovation of another space for the coming year. However, the center did have $15,000 in its bank account. Ms. Cooley had checked with L.C.A.'s Fiscal Department and determined that this $15,000 could be used towards a new site for the center.

She now had to decide which, if any, of these four buildings made the most sense from a financial point of view. She realized that one or more of them might not be financially possible.

One other factor complicating Ms. Cooley's decision was her long-time desire to expand the center from 28 to 40 children. It was with this in mind that she only looked at new buildings that could comfortably accommodate 40 children. Personally, she felt ready for the challenge of directing a larger program. She also wanted to respond to the obvious need in Lincoln for more early care and learning.

A final consideration was that expansion would allow her to diversify her population of children. She particularly wanted to include children with moderate special needs in the program.

In the past, her center found that each year there were several children enrolled who had previously unidentified special needs. The center always continued to serve these children, but never received any money for doing so, other than parent fees. Public dollars are not available unless the children are evaluated and identified as special needs children. Ten years ago, her center had held a license to accept up to seven children with special needs. The state no longer required such a license. She knew that under existing legislation she could contract with the Lincoln Public Schools to provide educational services for young children with identified special needs. In theory, the school department could pay the full tuition for the children. In practice, she wondered how easy it would be to identify such children in advance and enroll them at her center.

Exhibit 2

Lincoln Child Development Center

SUMMARY JOB DESCRIPTIONS

Director

Set educational philosophy and goals with head teachers; supervise center staff and operations; assure smooth administrative functioning of center; assist head teachers in developing curriculum; provide for in-service training of staff; assist parent coordinator in developing social service network and program.

Head Teacher

Develop curriculum and materials; plan and conduct activities; keep daily progress notes on individual children; set goals for children (with assistant teachers); assist in supervision of student teachers; participate in parent conferences.

Teacher

Plan and conduct activities; keep daily progress notes on individual children; set goals for children; participate in parent conferences.

Assistant Teacher

Plan and conduct daily activities for small and large groups; assist in conducting activities, in developing goals and keeping daily notes.

Parent Coordinator

Recruit and enroll eligible children; serve as liaison for families and staff with supportive social services; organize and encourage parent participation in center activities; promote communication between families and teaching staff.

Secretary

Provide typing and filing services to administrative and teaching personnel; organize and maintain parent/ teacher resource library; answer preliminary information requests regarding center; assist Director with ordering and bookkeeping.

Exhibit 3

Lincoln Child Development Center

Current Budget, July 1, 1996 - June 30, 1997

EXPENSES

Personnel

Director	$ 19,000
Parent coordinator	6,722
Head teacher	16,640
2 Co-teachers	30,950
Assistant teacher	15,320
1/2 Assistant teacher	7,936
1/2 Secretary	7,430
Fringes 20%	19,726
Substitutes	2,200
Custodian service	4,500
Consult and floater	10,334

Other Than Personnel

Classroom equipment	$ 1,400
Classroom supplies	1,200
Other supplies	560
Field trips	1,000
Rent	9,800
Utilities	3,844
Insurance	900
Maintenance	600
Office supplies	500
License	75
Printing	240
Telephone	1,200
Advertising	400
Travel	200
Postage, ADP	510
Staff training	500
Parent training	200
Audit	1,500

Total Personnel	$140,758	Total OTP	$ 24,629

	TOTAL EXPENSES	$165,387

INCOME

D.P.W. Donated Funds Contract (26 children)	$145,418
D.P.W. Direct Service Contract (2 children)	9,988
City of Lincoln Grant	20,000

	TOTAL INCOME	$175,406

Exhibit 4

Lincoln Child Development Center
Options for New Location

Building #1 — Rental

Capacity: 40 children. Rental: @ $200/month

Other: Needs additional $40,000 in renovations to bring it up to code and make it suitable for use as a children's center.

Building #2 — Rental

Capacity: 40 children. Rental: @ $2000/month

Other: Needs $6,000 worth of renovations to move in. Space is on 3 floors of a building.

Building #3 — Purchase

Capacity: 50 children. Purchase Price: $88,000

Other: Needs $6,000 worth of renovations.

Building #4 — Purchase

Capacity: 100 children. Purchase Price: $105,000

Other: Needs $40,000 worth of renovations, including new roof, new plumbing, and new heating. This is a three-story building, one story of which could be rented out as office space at $800/month.

Assignment: This center has four options, laid out on the previous page, but you are not asked to compare all four unless you want the work experience. For the purpose of detailed analysis, look at Rental option #1 and Purchase option #3.

For each of these two options, prepare a three-year budget projection for 1997-1998, 1998-1999, and 1999-2000. Make the following assumptions:

1. Assume that a final decision to rent or purchase could be made in the spring of 1997, and a move could take place on July 1, 1997.

2. For the sake of simplicity, assume a move could be made without having to stop operating the center for any period and, therefore, without any loss of income.

3. Assume that improvement loans are available from the bank at 12% interest, if co-signed by someone from L.C.A., with the loan repaid over five years.

4. For mortgages, assume that a 15% down payment would be required, and that a 20-year mortgage is available at 10%. (When you determine the size of the mortgage you need, call a local bank and ask what the monthly payments would be on such a mortgage, i.e., on a mortgage of x dollars at 10% for 20 years. There are tables with this information at the bank. In preparing your budget projections, remember to consider such factors as: increases in cost of living that affect other-than-personnel expenditures; potential raises in salaries for personnel, based on increased qualifications and length of service; utilization rates.

Which options do you prefer between the two — the rental or the purchase? Is this option preferable to keeping the program where it is? Given all the information in the case, and your three-year projections, what are some of your concerns about the future for this program?

8a. Southside Child Care: Deviation Analysis

In late May 1995, after careful consideration of three job opportunities, including interviews, visits, and discussions with people in the field, Steven Pearlman accepted a new position as Director of the Southside Children's Center, located just outside Nashville, TN. The position began on July 1, the beginning of the new fiscal year.

Several considerations prompted Steven to accept the Southside directorship. The center was located in a beautiful new facility, in an attractive, almost rural setting. He was especially interested in the program's protective service contract with the state that allowed eight children who were reported as being abused or neglected to receive free child care, regardless of the parents' financial situation. Steven had taken a course called "Children under Stress" and, as a project for his course, he had surveyed five Boston child care centers on their approach to child abuse and neglect — specifically, how they worked with children and with parents. Steven's previous experience of teaching, and his experience with one child in particular, had interested him in this issue. The emphasis on protective service at Southside excited him.

Steven moved to Tennessee during the first week in June and found an apartment about two miles from the center. He spent a week at the center, meeting with staff and children, and reviewing administrative details with the outgoing director.

Much of the discussion was devoted to budget. Steven had negotiated an annual salary for himself at $30,000. In addition, he had made two changes on the "income" side of the budget. By taking advantage of previously unrecognized contract provisions, Steven was able to increase the annual rate of food reimbursement significantly.

He also changed the amount of income budgeted under "private tuition" so that it was based, not on an assumption of full enrollment year-round, but rather on an assumption of 85% utilization over the year. He felt that this estimate for income was more likely to reflect the actual situation, as children came in and out of the center over the year.

Other minor changes were made in other budget categories. All revisions were discussed with and approved by the Board of Directors at a special meeting called in late June. Exhibit 1 is the center's previous budget through June 1995. The final annual budget for 1995-1996 as prepared by Steven and approved by the Board is Exhibit 2.

Exhibit 1

Southside Child Care

Operating Budget, January 1995 - June 1995

EXPENSES

Personnel		Other	
2 Head teachers	$ 27,586	Class supplies	$1,024
6 Teachers	43,972	Office supplies	616
Substitutes	2,464	Equipment	284
2 Protective service teachers	20,000	Phone	680
Director	16,000	Audit	1,000
Bookkeeper	3,498	Insurance	3,725
Cook	3,308	Food	14,000
Substitute	352	Rent	5,300
Nurse	3,194	Maintenance	1,840
Social worker	5,600	Transportation	5,400
Consultants	1,332	Miscellaneous	500
Fringe	6,245		
Driver	5,296		
(A)	**$138,847**	**(B)**	**$ 34,369**

TOTAL EXPENSES (A + B) $173,216

INCOME

Office for Children	$ 2,400
Welfare	90,104
Protective Services	52,632
County Commissioners	7,200
Food reimbursement	13,500
Private tuition	8,020
Southside Fund	1,400
TOTAL INCOME	**$175,256**
NET	**$ 2,040**

Exhibit 2

Southside Child Care

Operating Budget, July 1, 1995 - June 30, 1996

EXPENSES

Personnel		Other	
2 Head teachers	$ 43,680	Supplies	$ 2,050
6 Teachers	87,944	Office supplies	1,259
Substitutes	4,500	Classroom equipment	500
2 Protective service teachers	20,000	Phone	1,300
Director	30,000	Audit	1,000
Bookkeeper	7,000	Insurance	3,725
Cook	6,650	Food	28,000
Substitute	352	Rent	10,600
Nurse	6,400	Maintenance	4,000
Social worker	11,200	Transportation	11,000
Fringe @ 18%	32,692	Miscellaneous	1,000
Consultants	2,500		
Driver	10,600		
(A)	**$263,518**	**(B)**	**$ 64,434**

TOTAL EXPENSES (A + B) $327,952

INCOME

Office for Children	$ 4,800
Welfare	180,208
Protective Services	92,092
County Commissioners	14,400
Food reimbursement	20,000
Private tuition	16,040
Southside Fund	2,800
TOTAL INCOME	**$330,340**

Steven's first three months at Southside were no more or less eventful than he would have expected at any new job. Relations with staff and parents seemed to be going very well, and no major crises arose that Steven did not feel capable of handling. The multiple responsibilities of the new director's role were stimulating to him; he liked the fast pace, the frequent shifts to new challenges. He was surprised at how much conflict resolution he was called upon to do, and was trying to learn more about human relations.

The pace of the position, however, left him little time to think about budgets. Most financial decisions seemed to be made on an ad hoc basis. He was mildly frustrated to realize that the careful planning that had gone into his preparation of the annual budget was not reflected in the way financial decisions were being made.

Finally, in early October, Steven decided that he had to set aside a day to go over his budgets for the first three months. He wanted to see how close he was to the amounts that he had targeted for the program when he established the budget. He was concerned to see if any line items were significantly under or over budget, and to determine what steps might be necessary to deal with such situations.

On the morning of October 4, 1995, he met with the center's bookkeeper for an hour and a half. She reviewed for him all the financial activity of the center for each of the first three months. Steven's notes are reproduced on the next three pages as Exhibits 3, 4 and 5. He spent the rest of the day reviewing the data to try to determine how well he was sticking to his original budget.

Exhibit 3

Notes: Financial Activity in July 1995

INCOME

Sixteen children left the center at the end of June. During July,
ten were replaced immediately from the waiting list; one more was
replaced after seven days.

Actual income from welfare...................................... $8000

Actual income from private tuition $1670

All other actuals as budgeted.

EXPENSES

Teacher B, @ $15,000, was on paid vacation for 2 weeks.

Substitute was paid the minimum wage for 30 hours/week.

All other actual personnel expenses as budgeted.

Transportation: With changes in enrollment, only 4 children needed
transportation for a two-week period. Teachers picked them up.
Driver took unpaid vacation. Transportation costs up because of
multiple trips to community pool.

Actual expenses for driver....................................... $400

Actual expenses for transportation $585

Program: Arranged for children and staff to use community pool for
July through Labor Day @ one-time fee of $5/child and $10/adult.

Actual expenses $510

Supplies: Teachers purchased magic markers, construction paper,
several gallons of glue, etc.

Actual expenses for classroom supplies $300

Director made numerous phone calls to other centers around
North Carolina and Tennessee.

Actual phone expenses $201

Food costs down somewhat because of fewer children

Actual expenses for food $2016

Rent and maintenance as budgeted. No expenses in classroom
equipment, office supplies, audit, insurance, consultants.

Exhibit 4

Notes: Financial Activity in August 1995

Many children in and out; vacations affected reimbursements.

Actual income from welfare. $6960

Actual income from protective services $7520

Actual income from private tuition $1670

All other income as budgeted.

Staff took unpaid vacations because so few children at Center.
One teacher took one-month leave.

Actual expenses for Teacher A $0

Actual expenses for Teacher B. $760

Actual expenses for Lead Teacher A $1100

Cook took 3 weeks paid vacation

Substitute cook hired 20 hours/week @ $9.00/hour

Actual expenses for substitute cook $540

All other personnel actual costs were spent as budgeted.

Insurance bill for year came in 8% higher than expected
because of claim made last year, when all of the outdoor
equipment was stolen from the yard.

Actual expense for insurance. $4010

Head teacher replenished first aid box, bought yarn and
dyes for weaving project, etc.

Actual expenses for class supplies $170

No classroom equipment bought; no actuals in audit
or miscellaneous. Rent and maintenance as budgeted.

Actual expenses for office supplies (stamps) $30

Actual expenses for phone $179

Actual expenses for food. $990

Actual expenses for transportation $575

Workshop NewGames Foundation.

Actual expenses for consultants $200

Exhibit 5

Notes: Financial Activity in September 1995

INCOME

Center fully enrolled after Labor Day. Private tuitions close to capacity.

Actual income from private tuition $835

All other actuals as budgeted.

EXPENSES

Much staff overtime because of enrollment of new children;
one Saturday for painting center.

Actual expenses for Teacher A. $2000

Actual expenses for Teacher B. $2200

Actual expenses for Teacher C. $2275

Actual expenses for 2 Protective Services Teachers, each $800

Actual expenses for bookkeeper $450

All other actual personnel costs are as budgeted.

Consultant psychiatrist to meet weekly with protective service
teacher, @ $100/week.

Actual expenses for consultants $500

Heavy purchases of paint, paper, glue, scissors, etc. at
Annual Teachers Warehouse Sale.

Actual expenses for classroom supplies $1216

Purchased different shapes of blocks to add to center's set.

Actual expenses for classroom equipment $200

New center stationery purchased; new stamp with the
center's logo. New word processing software.

Actual expenses for office supplies $535

Actual expenses for phone $202

Actual expenses for food $2200

Rent as budgeted.

No expenses in audit, insurance, or miscellaneous.

Maintenance costs went up as of September.

Actual expenses for maintenance $800

Actual expenses for transportation $500

Assignment: Prepare a budget deviation analysis, using either a computer spreadsheet, or ledger paper, with at least 13 columns. Follow the steps below. Write a narrative description of what the deviations are, and what you think any of them might mean. How serious might they be? If any are not serious, why not? Stepping into Steven's shoes, what will you, the director, do about them, if anything?

Overview summary: four steps in a budget deviation

1. Convert your annual budget into monthly budgets for the three months covered in the assignment.

2. Compare what was planned, for both income and expense, with actual income and expense in each of those months.

3. Consider the implications that any changes in actual income and expenditures for those three months might have for the remainder of the budget, the coming 9 months.

4. Write your narrative analysis.

A step-by-step how-to summary for budget deviation

Sharpen your pencil, get out your calculator, spread out your ledger paper or boot up your spreadsheet software, then read the following step-by-step how-to instructions.

> *Convert your annual budget into monthly budgets* for the three months covered in the assignment. Divide the budget into twelve monthly budgets, and use three of them for July, August and September.

The purpose of the first step is to figure out a monthly budget for three specific months — July, August and September — using your annual budget, 1995-1996. Read the following instructions for Step 1. If you understand how to create the monthly budget information you need and how to use that information to think about the remaining 9 months, skip step 1 and move to step 2.

STEP ONE

To prepare monthly budgets, use ledger paper or a computer.

a. List each of the line items in the left-hand column, making a line for each of your sub-totals and totals.

b. Label column 13 "ANNUAL TOTAL" and put the annual amount for each item in that column.

c. Label column 1 "July," column 2 "August" and column 3 "September." Label column 4, "9 months" and put all the rest of the budget for

October-June in this column. Or, if you prefer, label all the 12 columns with the name of a month, and show a monthly budget for each month.

d. Allocate for each line item an amount for July, August, and September in Columns 1, 2, and 3. Figure out when you think the amounts might be spent. The easiest way to do it is to consider each month to be 1/12 of the budget.

e. For this case, you are asked to consider activity in July, August and September, so there is no need to spend a lot of time worrying about how to spread costs in months 4-12 if you don't want to.

However you do it, understand that for each line item in your itemized left-hand column, the amounts in columns 1-12 will add up to the total budgeted annual amount, in column 13.

STEP TWO

Using a second piece of ledger paper or a new spreadsheet in your computer, follow these steps. As before, you need to list line items and have 13 or more columns.

a. Same as step one.

b. Same as step one.

c. Label your columns on this second page as follows. Label column 1 "BUDGETED," column 2 "ACTUAL," column 3 "DEVIANCE." Leave column 4 blank. Bracket and label these 4 columns at the top of your page to indicate that they are all for the month of July.

d. Label columns 5-8 with the same 4 labels, bracketing and labeling them as August. Bracket and label columns 9-12 with the same 4 labels for September.

e. Leave column 13 blank.

f. From your first worksheet, enter the budgeted amount for each line, for each month, in the columns you have labeled "BUDGETED" (columns 1, 5, and 9, for July, August and September).

g. In column 2, enter the ACTUAL amount spent on each line item in July.

h. In column 3, enter the difference between column 1 and column 2. If the difference is NOT in the center's favor and the item is overspent, put it in parentheses, or precede it with a minus sign.

For example, if the center budgeted $100 for supplies, and spent $101, you will enter $100 in column 1, $101 in column 2. You will enter into the third column ($1) or - $1. If the center expected to receive $500 from the Office for Children, but actually received only $300, you will enter those two numbers in the Actual and in the Budgeted columns and into column 3, ($200) or - $200.

i. Repeat the same process for August and September, using the columns labeled "ACTUAL" for what was really spent, and the columns labeled "DEVIANCE" for the difference between budgeted expenditures and actual expenditures.

Think about each of the deviances you have found. List them, and write a narrative discussion of each, explaining why you think action is needed or not needed. Note: We've left column 4 blank in the budget deviation analysis for you to use in any way you want. You can make notes, put in symbols signaling action, or whatever you like. Or you might want to use the column to give a percentage to the deviation. This could be done in one of several ways.

NOTE ON PERCENTAGES:

1. You can express column 3 (deviance) as a percentage of column 1 (budgeted). For example, if you budgeted $500, but you only spent $400, you have a deviance of 20%; what you spent deviated by 20% from what you planned to spend.

2. You can express column 2 (actual) as a percentage of column 1 (budgeted). For example, if you budgeted $500, but you only spent $400, you spent 80% of the monthly amount budgeted. Most items would be 100%, and you would be interested in percentages above or below 100%.

3. You can express column 2 (monthly actual) as a percentage of column 13 (annual budgeted). For example, if an item was budgeted for the year at $1200, but you spent in one month $210, you would show this in column 4 as 17.5%. Most of the expenditures would be 1/12, a percentage of 8.33%, so percentages above and below that would be of interest to you.

STEP THREE

This step requires you to think about what these deviances mean, and to write a narrative describing what you would do about each one. You can skip step 3 if you think you can use column 4 of Step 2 to give you further information from which you can write such a narrative. If you skip step 3, go straight to the Narrative Discussion.

To consider what these changes mean for the remainder of the year, take a third piece of ledger paper, or start a new spreadsheet.

a. Same as in step one.

b. Same as in step one.

c. Cumulate the July-September budgeted amount in column 1, a 3-months budget for each line item.

d. Cumulate the actual July-September expenditures in column 2 for each line item.

e. Cumulate the deviance for each line item in column 3.

f. Skip a column.

g. Cumulate a 9-months budget, October-June in column 5.

h. Using whatever format makes sense to you, make notes or fill in columns to compare the 9-months budget with what happened in July-September.

Narrative Discussion

What is your thinking about any deviances you found?

If there is a surplus, what are your plans?

Are there over-expenditures? Are these serious problems or not? Will you do anything about them or not?

For example, what are you going to do about the phone bill?

Is the expenditure for the cook a problem?

What is your thinking about the food budget? transportation?

What are your options for dealing with items where costs have increased?

What about the anticipated income?

8b. Projections of Personnel Costs at Southside

Steven enjoyed doing the deviation analysis, and he instructed the book-keeper to prepare this information for him once a month. He felt he understood the expenditure side of his budget and current decisions about spending. However, he wanted to be able to think clearly about the future. He was planning a 4% increase for all staff in the coming year. He wondered what the budget would look like a few years down the road if he were to increase salaries every year.

Assignment: You are Steven. Using ledger paper with three columns or a spreadsheet on your computer, prepare a projected staffing budget. Project staff costs for the current year (1995-1996), and the next two years, using the first column for the current budget, the second column for next year, and the third for the year after next. This budget includes only your personnel expenditures. Exhibit 1 and Exhibit 2 in the Southside Case (8a) above have the budget detail you will need.

As Steven, would you try to make across-the-board increases every year for all staff, to reflect cost of living? What is the cost of living? Does the cost of living actually go up every year? What are the implications of your decision? Do you have other alternatives? See Fairchild salary schedule on page 33 of this book.

9. Martin Luther King Child Care Center

Part A: Background

Memorial Hospital began to develop a strong interest in health programs for outpatient children during the 1960s. Funds were found for a treatment program for physically handicapped children, and an Executive Program Director was employed, Dr. Lois Pineby. Pineby was talented, ambitious, and intensely dedicated to her work. The program grew in size over the next few years, and was found to be extremely effective.

During this period, Pineby began to identify other program areas where there were needs, and to write proposals for funding additional programs for children at the hospital. A Health Screening program, an infant program that provided home visitors for retarded children, and a play program for hospital patients were all developed.

By 1969, the hospital was operating five different children's programs, with multiple funding sources. Pineby had administrative responsibility for them all. The heads of each program reported to her; she approved budget expenditures and helped obtain funding, coordinated shared services (such as the use of consultants), and oversaw the accounting for each program in the central hospital business office.

In 1969, Title IV-A of the federal Social Security Act made large amounts of funds available to the states for child care. The funds were available on a 75:25%-matching basis. The federal government would provide 75% of the funds, and the state had to find the 25% matching funds. The matching, or non-federal share of the money came either from state tax dollars or from local communities. Most states appropriated the entire amount they wished to spend in their state budget, and then claimed federal reimbursement for 75% of what they spent. If a state was not willing to pay the entire 25% to draw down the federal dollars, it could ask for a local "match."

Pineby's state embarked on a massive increase in child care programs. Sometimes the 25% match was covered with state funds, and sometimes the matching funds came from local "umbrella" agencies. Programs were funded by the state's Department of Public Welfare (DPW). State funds went to regional DPW Offices. Each regional office would negotiate a Prime Contract in each county, or combination of counties. These Prime Contractors became "umbrella" funding organizations, negotiating sub-contracts with agencies that operate the child care programs. The Prime

Contractor provided the "local share" and the state provided the "state share" of the income, so that the centers that were funded were not responsible for any matching.

Children served had to meet eligibility requirements established by state and federal guidelines: parental income had to be at a poverty level, and the primary caregiver of the child had to be employed or in school. Pineby had developed a proposal for a day care center at the hospital, using these funds. The center was to serve neighborhood children and children of hospital staff. The neighborhood children, all low-income, were to be funded by DPW, and the staff children would be paid for by parent fees, on a sliding scale basis.

Since Pineby had long been concerned with handicapped children, she saw the day care center as preventive. The center would serve children "at risk" — children who might later need treatment, but whose problems might be ameliorated through early identification and prevention. A significant number of teenage mothers lived in the urban community served by the hospital. The center's hospital wanted to serve children from birth until public school entry.

Memorial Hospital became one of the sub-contractors and agreed under a contract with the Prime Contractor, or umbrella agency, to provide service for 35 children.

Part B: The Child Care Center
The Center opened in the spring of 1971. Because of the need to fill the allocated slots quickly, children were admitted to the center essentially on a first-come, first-served basis, with scant attention paid to the financial requirements of the government or the "at risk" designation under which the center had originally been conceived and funded. The hospital was located in a low-income area where residents were assumed to be "at risk."

During its first year, the Center had to move twice. Quarters had been found hastily, and proved unworkable. A new location, near the hospital, was found and renovated. After several months there, a fire forced the center to relocate once again. At that point, they moved to an old church near the hospital, and took over what had been the educational wing of the church. Office space was shared with church personnel, and the Sunday school used several of the classrooms.

The main staff of the center initially consisted of an Infant Head Teacher and Assistants, a Toddler Head Teacher and Assistants, and a Center Director-Teacher in the Preschool Room with Assistants. This structure proved unfeasible, and the Center Director soon moved into a full-time, non-teaching position. A third Head Teacher was hired for the Preschool Room. A Social Worker and part-time consultants shared across the other hospital programs run by Pineby, were also part of the staffing of the program.

The Director, concerned with building a staff, moving and improving space, ordering supplies and materials, and developing a program, remained uninvolved in the fundraising and financial aspects of the Center. Pineby took care of these aspects of the operation.

In the spring of 1973, the Director left. The Social Worker, who had been with the center almost from the beginning, continued working until the following September, serving in a dual role as Social Worker and Acting Director.

At the end of August, 1973, no replacement for the Director had been found. The Social Worker resigned effective September 1973. Things at the Center were now in very bad shape. There were bad feelings among the staff, and a great deal of staff turnover, lateness, and absenteeism. Attendance of children was down, and parents were disgruntled. The building was dirty and in need of many minor repairs and safety features. Supplies were low or nonexistent. Funding had been approved only until the end of October, due to problems with the State Legislature's appropriation for the overall state budget.

During the summer, the consulting psychologist wrote a confidential memo to Pineby saying that, in her opinion, conditions at the center were so bad that if a Director were not found almost immediately, the center ought to be closed. She reported unsafe conditions with cleaning products accessible to children, staff sleeping on the job, children left unattended, inadequate supervision of children during parts of the day, and other problems.

Sue Barker was referred to Pineby as a candidate for the Director's job by one of Pineby's colleagues. Pineby and Barker, who had never met, spoke briefly on the phone, and Pineby set up a date when she, staff and parents would all be able to interview Barker. Here is Barker's report of that day.

Barker's Report: *I knew before I went in that I had the job if I wanted it, and was very excited about it. I knew that I'd been highly recommended for the job, and that they were badly in need of a Center Director. (I didn't find out how badly until later!)*

Dr. Pineby and I talked, and it immediately became evident that she was deeply involved in the workings of the day care center — more so than seemed appropriate to me, considering her position as coordinator of a number of different programs.

I then was taken over to the Center to walk around and talk informally to staff people on the playground. I talked mainly to the Toddler and Preschool Head Teachers. I was very impressed with what they both said about their philosophy and about the center's programs.

Later, during naptime, the staff gathered in the Infant Room so everyone could get a chance to hear from me and ask questions. At that session, my earlier suspicions about Pineby's strong role were confirmed. There was a great deal of concern about who would be making decisions, since, they said, the previous director always had to ask Pineby's permission to do anything, and decisions she made on her own were often countermanded by Pineby. The previous director never seemed to know how much money they had to spend, the staff said. They also expressed a great deal of concern with where I would see the director's responsibility. They said that the previous director had never been around, which created a real vacuum and lots of problems. They also asked about the role that I felt parents should play in the Center.

I told them that my concept of the director's job was to do everything possible to free the teachers from external hassles so that they could concentrate on what they were hired to do - care for children. I also told them that I didn't know where else I would be, and of course expected to be physically present at the center. (I later found out just how difficult this was to do much of the time.) I told them I might be interested in organizing the classrooms in cross-age family groupings rather than by age group; they were politely noncommittal about that idea. I was also quite explicit about my feelings about parent involvement, since I knew that if I weren't, there would be problems later. I told them I felt we were here caring for other people's children, and that those were the people for whom we were, or should be, working. I said that I saw extensive parent involvement ultimately leading to complete parent control of the center. I said that one of our jobs would be to communicate to the parents why we were doing what we did at the Center, and how we were accomplishing the parents' goals for their children.

Later, I was interviewed by the parents. This group, which I had visualized as a large, organized body, turned out to be three parents, one of them also a staff member. They had two concerns — whether I would continue to have boys and girls share the same bathroom, and whether I would continue to send the children outside for an hour every afternoon even if the weather was cold.

Barker left the office with a copy of the Proposal for the 12-month budget (Exhibit 1) that Pineby had written and expected to be funded for the current year, before a budget crisis in the Legislature resulted in only partial funding.

She also took away with her the approved 4-month budget (Exhibit 2) under which the center was then operating because the Legislature had not yet approved the state's budget for the year. She also had a draft of the 8-month budget Pineby had prepared for the center and planned to submit in less than two weeks to the Prime Contractor (Exhibit 3). This 8-month budget would cover the center for the remainder of the year. It was not yet neatly typed, but Pineby considered it in final form. Barker went home to try to sort it all out.

There was a week between her interviews and the starting date for the job. Barker tentatively accepted the position, but she told Pineby that she had some reservations that she intended to resolve at once. The next day, Barker spent more time at the center talking with the outgoing Social Worker who had been acting as Director during the past few months. She also observed in classrooms, and attended a weekly "staff conference."

The staff conferences were attended by as many of the staff as could come, depending upon how many children there were in the center at the time. Consultants from the hospital who worked with the center also attended, including a pediatrician, nurse, psychologist, speech therapist, and nutritionist. The meetings were held in the hospital in the pediatrician's office, and were led by the psychologist. The purpose of the conferences was to discuss individual children, and some attempts had been made to set up a schedule of conferences and follow-up discussions on children about whom teachers had concerns.

While Barker was visiting the program, she had a call from Pineby. Pineby informed Barker that she (Pineby) had some concerns about the Preschool Head Teacher. Debby Stoner, the teacher, was still in her probationary period, standard for all employees of the hospital during the first three months of employment. Pineby thought that perhaps she should not be kept on. Pineby offered to fire Stoner before Barker started as Director, to save Barker the difficulty in parent and staff relations that might ensue. Barker told Pineby not to do anything, and said that she (Barker) would spend some time in Stoner's classroom in order to make the decision herself. Pineby warned that the probationary period expired in mid-October, so that the decision would have to be made quickly.

Part C: Budgeting

There obviously were an almost unlimited number of urgent priorities that could be identified at the center. To Barker, among the most urgent was the budget. The previous director had left most of the budget work and financial management to Pineby, and therefore had no actual control of the budget for her own program. Whenever she tried to make any decisions, she was stymied by her limited role in the budget process.

Barker knew that she would have to get a handle on the budget situation quickly. She learned that the State had approved 4-month contracts that year for all Title IV-A contracted child care centers, rather than annual contracts. The reason was that the State Legislature had adjourned for the summer without agreeing on the annual state budget, and had appropriated only enough to cover expenditures through October. The Legislature was now back and working on the passage of the budget. The remainder of the money would be available, but a new budget for November through June had to be submitted to the Prime Contractor within a few weeks.

Pineby, working with a hospital accountant in the central business office as she had always done in the past, had quickly drawn up an 8-month budget to submit. Her final figure was in the "ballpark" of what they had been told could ultimately be approved. Barker saw writing this 8-month budget herself as an excellent opportunity to write the budget that would guide her work for most of the year.

She set to work. In addition to digging through all the documents available to her (See Exhibits 1-5), she gathered official and unofficial information from talks with various people. The following day, she spoke with the accountant in the hospital business office. From the hospital, she made some calls to the Prime Contractor and the Regional State DPW office. She also spoke again with the outgoing social worker, gathering all the information she could about the budget.

She found out there was a serious disagreement between the hospital and the Prime Contractor on the amount of consulting services needed. The Prime Contractor wanted consulting services cut way back. Pineby wanted to keep them as high as possible for three reasons: (1) to provide the interdisciplinary services she felt the children needed; (2) to help her meet commitments made to consultants who were working for a number of Pineby's programs; and, in a few cases, (3) to show an in-kind budget item contributed by hospital funds that could match federal or state money in contracts other than the child care contract.

The number of substitutes the Prime Contractor would allow exceeded the actual number needed, since substitutes were not always called when a caregiver was absent, depending on the absenteeism of children. Also, the amount the Prime Contractor would allow for substitute pay was higher than the Center actually paid by $2/hour.

She was told that employee benefits should be enumerated for the budget to be approved, and that the basis for cost analysis on salaries and all items had to be explained much more clearly. She was told to include tuition remission costs in the budget if any employees would be taking courses (see Exhibit 4), since the hospital's Personnel Department had discovered that they had been reimbursing the center's staff for tuition without specific funds included in the budget to cover that cost. Travel needed to be broken down into local and out-of-town travel for parents, staff, and children.

Although the actual cost for food was 55 1/2 cents per day per child, Barker was told by the Prime Contractor they could spend more. The amount in this budget category could be raised. She was told to itemize the utilities under the space category, and to move maintenance costs to personnel.

She was also told that the costs of Administrative Overhead could be as high as 12%, since the Hospital provided many services (office supplies, security, laundry, etc.) that are usually budgeted as line items and not usually included in overhead. The 12% percentage had previously been approved under a different federal contract as a maximum limit for overhead on the hospital's projects, but Pineby was charging less to the state in her child care contract.

Whatever changes she made in the budget, Barker was told to be sure to stay within the ballpark figure that had already been tentatively approved in the draft of the 4-month budget (Exhibit 2). That budget was based on the 12-month budget that was approved, but not funded (because of the failure of the Legislature to appropriate a budget). With all of these additional directions and options, Barker struggled to read the poorly mimeographed and confusingly numbered budgets and the pages of regulations (guidelines) for the proposal supplied by the Prime Contractor.

Barker made a late-afternoon telephone call to the licensing agency's main office in the state capital before she left for the day. "What I'd really like to do, although it may not be possible," she said, "is to set up a family-like grouping with infants, toddlers, and preschoolers, instead of the usual grouping by age. I'd like to know whether you'd permit this on a demonstration basis." Barker wanted one staff person to be responsible for one infant, two toddlers, and three preschoolers. The licensing office preferred a pattern of two staff people for one infant, three toddlers and five preschoolers. Barker felt that the 9/2 grouping would clearly be approved, and that she could get her preferred pattern of 6/1 if she could make a good case for it. She would make her decision among the different options for staffing for the center's 9-hour day before making her budget.

Barker's last act for the day was to call Pineby's office to make an appointment for 3:00 p.m. the next afternoon, leaving free her evening and all the next morning to produce a new budget.

Assignment: As Sue Barker, do you want this job? What problems have you uncovered at the center? What will you say to Pineby when you meet with her? How will she react? Prepare the budget material that you will discuss with her. Think about whether the budget you are preparing addresses the problems Barker found at the center.

Guide to Exhibits: Martin Luther King

Exhibit 1 shows the initial 12-month budget submitted along with the Proposal for the year between July 1, 1973 to June 30, 1974. The budget has eight categories. It was submitted in February 1973, and approved by the local Prime Contractor. However, this budget was not funded because the Legislature did not agree on the total state budget before July 1, 1973. When the state Legislature failed to appropriate the state budget in time, all day care agencies receiving these funds were directed to break down their budgets into a 4-month budget and an 8-month budget. The 4-month budget was funded while the Legislature continued to debate the state budget all summer. NOTE: Category VIII, "DPW Administrative Costs," sets a flat 1/19 of the total cost of Categories I - VII. This money is a percentage of the total budget that DPW can claim in federal reimbursement for its own costs of administering the funding program. No part of these costs must be paid by the center. Note also: the "local share" is the responsibility of the Prime Contractor, not the center. The total for categories I-VII is the center's budget.

Exhibit 2 shows the approved 4-month budget for the period from July 1, 1973 through October 31, 1973. The 4-month budget was to be approximately 1/3 of the originally submitted 12-month budget, except that expenditures in the "Equipment" category were to be deleted. This budget has the same eight categories used by the state for budget proposals.

Exhibit 3 shows the subsequent working copy of the 8-month budget for the remainder of the year, drawn up by Pineby with the central budget office of the Hospital in the absence of a day care center Director. A final 8-month budget had to be submitted by the end of September 1973. The total amount of the 4-month budget (Exhibit 2) and the 8-month budget had to equal approximately the amount of the initial 12-month proposed budget (Exhibit 1).

Exhibit 4 summarizes the hospital's personnel policies.

Exhibit 5 is a note on Title IV-A, Title XX, CCDBG, and other sources of governmental funds.

Exhibit 1

Martin Luther King Child Care Center (MLKCCC)
12-Month Budget (Submitted 2/73)

CATEGORY	ITEM	LOCAL	STATE	TOTAL
I	Personnel	$ 5,061	$ 94,360	$ 99,421
II	Consultants & contract services	12,159	0	12,159
III	Travel	0	1,000	1,000
IV	Consumable supplies	1,600	5,005	6,605
V	Equipment & furniture	2,000	0	2,000
VI	Space	3,800	3,000	6,800
VII	Other costs	12,410	331	12,741
VIII	DPW Administrative	0	7,406	7,406
GRAND TOTAL		**$37,030**	**$111,102**	**$148,132**

Exhibit 1

MLKCCC — 12-Month Budget, Categories I-VIII

CATEGORY I: PERSONNEL

A. Full-time Personnel

# OF PERSONS	POSITION OR TITLE	% TIME ON PROJECT	MONTHS EMPLOYED	LOCAL	STATE	TOTAL
1	Director	100	12	0	$12,669	$12,669
3	Supervisor/	100	12	0	22,658	22,658
	child care workers	100	12	0	17,409	17,409
1	Cook	100	12	0	5,275	5,275
1	Social worker	100	12	0	9,284	9,284
Subtotal					$67,295	$67,295

B. Part-time Personnel

# OF PERSONS	POSITION OR TITLE	% TIME ON PROJECT	MONTHS EMPLOYED	LOCAL	STATE	TOTAL
5	Child care workers	50	12	0	$14,510	$14,510
1	Social work aide	50	12	2,500	0	2,500
1	Secretary	50	12	2,561	1,237	3,798
	Substitutes*			–	2,280	2,280
Subtotal				$ 5,061	$18,027	$23,088
Fringe Benefits				0	9,038	9,038
TOTAL CATEGORY I: PERSONNEL				**$ 5,061**	**$94,360**	**$99,421**

*Substitutes

3 Head teachers, 10 days each @ $25/day	$750
18 days illness and training @ $25/day	450
5 Assistant teachers, 10 days @ $18/day	900
10 days illness and training @ $18/day	180

Exhibit 1

MLKCCC — 12-Month Budget, Categories I-VIII continued

CATEGORY II: CONSULTANT AND CONTRACT SERVICES

SPECIALIST	BASIS FOR COST ESTIMATE	LOCAL	STATE	TOTAL
Program consultant	7 1/2 hrs/wk @ $10.55/hr x 42 wks	$ 3,323	$ 0	$ 3,323
Psychology	5 hrs/wk @ $10.55/hr x 42 wks	2,216	0	2,216
Speech & language	5 hrs/wk @ $10.55/hr x 42 wks	2,216	0	2,216
Pediatric	35 children @ $52.75 per child	1,846	0	1,846
Nutrition	4 hrs/wk @ $8.30/hr x 50 wks	1,661	0	1,661
Nurse	17 days @ $52.75/day	897	0	897
TOTAL CATEGORY II: CONSULTANT & CONTRACT SERVICES		**$12,159**	**$ 0**	**$12,159**

CATEGORY III: TRAVEL

ITEM	BASIS FOR COST ESTIMATE	LOCAL	STATE	TOTAL
Training & conferences	Staff and parents 5-10 staff and 5-10 parents @ 3 sessions each @ $25		$ 500	$ 500
Field trips	Parents, staff and children (12 trips @ $40/trip) including food and transportation for 15 children, 15 parents + 4 staff @ $1/person		500	500
TOTAL CATEGORY III: TRAVEL			**$ 1,000**	**$ 1,000**

CATEGORY IV: CONSUMABLE SUPPLIES

ITEM	BASIS FOR COST ESTIMATE	LOCAL	STATE	TOTAL
Food	Avg. 55.5 cents/day x 35 children	$ 0	$ 5,005	$ 5,005
Supplies	10 infants/10 toddlers	650	0	650
Supplies	15 preschoolers x 260 days	950	0	950
TOTAL CATEGORY IV: CONSUMABLE SUPPLIES		**$ 1,600**	**$ 5,005**	**$ 6,605**

Exhibit 1

MLKCCC — 12-Month Budget, Categories I-VIII continued

CATEGORY V: EQUIPMENT AND FURNITURE

ITEM	BASIS FOR COST ESTIMATE	LOCAL	STATE	TOTAL
Equipment	For 15 children	$ 2,000	$ 0	$ 2,000
TOTAL CATEGORY V: EQUIPMENT AND FURNITURE		$ 2,000	$ 0	$ 2,000

CATEGORY VI: SPACE

ITEM	BASIS FOR COST ESTIMATE	LOCAL	STATE	TOTAL
Center space	3,000 sq.ft. @ $1/sq.ft./yr.	$ 0	$ 3,000	$ 3,000
Utilities	Based on previous experience	3,800	0	3,800
Maintenance				
TOTAL CATEGORY VI: SPACE		$ 3,800	$ 3,000	$ 6,800

CATEGORY VII: OTHER COSTS

ITEM	BASIS FOR COST ESTIMATE	LOCAL	STATE	TOTAL
Overhead	10% of personnel	$ 9,942	$ 0	$ 9,942
Telephone	Installation & use	419	331	750
Printing		250		250
Postage		899		899
Insurance		750		750
Books, etc.		150		150
TOTAL CATEGORY VII: OTHER COSTS		$12,410	$ 331	$ 12,741

CATEGORY VIII: DPW ADMINISTRATION COSTS

ITEM	BASIS FOR COST ESTIMATE	LOCAL	STATE	TOTAL
	1/19 of total program costs categories I - VII			
	1/19 of $140,726			
TOTAL CATEGORY VIII: DPW COSTS		$ 0	$ 7,406	$ 7,406

GRAND TOTAL - LOCAL SHARE		$ 37,030
GRAND TOTAL - STATE SHARE		$ 111,102
GRAND TOTAL - PROJECT		$ 148,132

Exhibit 2

MLKCCC — Approved 4-Month Budget

CATEGORY	ITEM	LOCAL	STATE	TOTAL
I	Personnel	$6,230	$18,692	$24,922
II	Consultants and contract services	960	2,881	3,841
III	Travel	84	250	334
IV	Consumable supplies	556	1,668	2,224
V	Equipment & furniture	0	0	0
VI	Space	567	1,700	2,267
VII	Other costs	856	2,569	3,425
VIII	DPW Administrative	487	1,461	1,948
GRAND TOTAL		$9,740	$29,221	$38,961

Exhibit 2

MLKCCC — 4-Month Budget, Categories I-VIII

CATEGORY I: PERSONNEL

Full-time Personnel

# OF PERSONS	POSITION OR TITLE	% TIME ON PROJECT	MONTHS EMPLOYED	TOTAL
1	Director	100	4	$ 3,769
3	Supervisor/teachers	100	4	5,910
3	Child care workers	100	4	3,461
1	Cook	100	4	1,629
1	Social worker	100	4	2,132

Part-time Personnel

# OF PERSONS	POSITION OR TITLE	% TIME ON PROJECT	MONTHS EMPLOYED	TOTAL
5	Child care workers	50	4	$ 2,885
0	Social work aide	0	0	0
1	Secretary	50	4	1,266
	Substitutes			525
Subtotal				$21,577
5.5% Salary Increase				1,187
Fringe Benefits 10%				2,158
TOTAL CATEGORY I: PERSONNEL				**$24,922**

CATEGORY II: CONSULTANT AND CONTRACT SERVICES

SPECIALISTS	BASIS FOR COST ESTIMATE	TOTAL
Program consultant	7 1/2 hrs/wk @ $10/hr x 14 wks	$ 1,050
Psychology	5 hrs/wk @ $10/hr x 14 wks	700
Speech & language	5 hrs/wk @ $10/hr x 14 wks	700
Pediatric	12 children @ $50/child	600
Nutrition	4 hrs/wk @ $8/hr x 16.4 wks	524
Nurse	@ $50/day	267
TOTAL CATEGORY II: CONSULTANT & CONTRACT SERVICES		**$ 3,841**

Exhibit 2

MLKCCC — 4-Month Budget, Categories I-VIII continued

CATEGORY III: TRAVEL

ITEM	BASIS FOR COST ESTIMATE	TOTAL
Training & conferences	Staff and parents 5-10 staff and 5-10 parents @ 1 session each @ $24	$ 167
Field Trips	Parents, staff and children (4 trips @ $40/trip) including food and transportation for 15 children, 15 parents & 4 staff @ $1.23 each	167
TOTAL CATEGORY III: TRAVEL		**$ 334**

CATEGORY IV: CONSUMABLE SUPPLIES

ITEM	BASIS FOR COST ESTIMATE	TOTAL
Food	Avg. 55.5 cents/day x 35 children x 87 days	$ 1,690
Supplies	10 infants/10 toddlers	234
Supplies	15 preschoolers x 87 days	300
Needed office supplies will be provided through the hospital.		
TOTAL CATEGORY IV: CONSUMABLE SUPPLIES		**$ 2,224**

CATEGORY V: EQUIPMENT AND FURNITURE

ITEM	BASIS FOR COST ESTIMATE	TOTAL
Equipment		$ 0
TOTAL CATEGORY V: EQUIPMENT		**$ 0**

CATEGORY VI: SPACE

ITEM	BASIS FOR COST ESTIMATE	TOTAL
Space	3,000 sq.ft. @ $1/sq.ft./yr./4-month period	$ 1,000
Utilities and maintenance	Based on previous experience	1,267
TOTAL CATEGORY VI: SPACE		**$ 2,267**

Exhibit 2

MLKCCC — 4-Month Budget, Categories I-VIII continued

CATEGORY VII: OTHER COSTS

ITEM	BASIS FOR COST ESTIMATE	TOTAL
Overhead	@ 10% of personnel	$ 2,492
Telephone	Installation & use	250
Printing		83
Insurance		133
Subscriptions, books, etc.		50
Miscellaneous, postage		417
TOTAL CATEGORY VII: OTHER COSTS		$ 3,425

CATEGORY VIII: DPW ADMINISTRATIVE COSTS

ITEM	BASIS FOR COST ESTIMATE	TOTAL
	1/19 of total program costs categories I - VII	
	1/19 of $37,013	
TOTAL CATEGORY VIII: DPW ADMINISTRATIVE COSTS		$ 1,948

GRAND TOTAL - LOCAL SHARE	$ 9,740
GRAND TOTAL - STATE SHARE	$ 29,221
GRAND TOTAL - PROJECT	$ 38,961

Exhibit 3

MLKCCC — Working Copy 8-Month Budget, Pineby

CATEGORY	ITEM	LOCAL	STATE	TOTAL
I	Personnel	$18,613	$55,839	$ 74,452
II	Consultants and contract services	1,921	5,763	7,684
III	Travel	167	499	666
IV	Consumable supplies	1,121	3,364	4,485
V	Equipment & furniture	500	1,500	2,000
VI	Space	1,133	3,400	4,533
VII	Other costs	2,348	7,044	9,392
VIII	DPW Administrative	1,358	4,074	5,432
GRAND TOTAL		$27,161	$81,483	$108,644

Exhibit 3

MLKCCC — 8-Month Budget, Pineby Breakdown

CATEGORY I: PERSONNEL

Full-time Personnel

# OF PERSONS	POSITION OR TITLE	% TIME ON PROJECT	MONTHS EMPLOYED	TOTAL
1	Director	100	8	$ 8,684
3	Supervisor/teachers	100	8	16,423
3	Child care workers	100	8	13,758
1	Cook	100	8	3,556
1	Social worker	100	8	7,035

Part-time Personnel

# OF PERSONS	POSITION OR TITLE	% TIME ON PROJECT	MONTHS EMPLOYED	TOTAL
5	Child care workers	50	8	$ 11,466
1	Social work aide	50	8	2,500
1	Secretary	50	8	2,462
	Substitutes			1,800
Subtotal				$ 67,684
Fringe Benefits 10%				6,768
TOTAL CATEGORY: PERSONNEL				**$ 74,452**

CATEGORY II: CONSULTANT AND CONTRACT SERVICES

SPECIALISTS	BASIS FOR COST ESTIMATE	TOTAL
Program consultant	7 1/2 hrs/wk @ $10/hr x 28 wks	$ 2,100
Psychology	5 hrs/wk @ $10/hr x 28 wks	1,400
Speech & language	5 hrs/wk @ $10/hr x 28 wks	1,400
Pediatric	12 children @ $50/child	1,200
Nutrition	4 hrs/wk @ $8/hr x 32.8 wks	1,050
Nurse	@ $50/day	534
TOTAL CATEGORY II: CONSULTANT & CONTRACT SERVICES		**$ 7,684**

Exhibit 3

MLKCCC — 8-Month Budget, Pineby Breakdown continued

CATEGORY III: TRAVEL

ITEM	BASIS FOR COST ESTIMATE	TOTAL
Training & conferences	Staff and parents 5-10 staff and 5-10 parents @ 1 session each @ $24	$ 333
Field trips	Parents, staff and children (8 trips @ $40/trip) including food and transportation for 15 children, 15 parents & 4 staff @ $1.23 each	333
TOTAL CATEGORY III: TRAVEL		**$ 666**

CATEGORY IV: CONSUMABLE SUPPLIES

ITEM	BASIS FOR COST ESTIMATE	TOTAL
Food	Avg. 55.5 cents/day x 35 children x 176 days	$3,419
Supplies	10 infants/10 toddlers	433
Supplies	15 preschoolers x 176 days	633
Office supplies will be provided by hospital.		
TOTAL CATEGORY IV: CONSUMABLE SUPPLIES		**$4,485**

CATEGORY V: EQUIPMENT AND FURNITURE

ITEM	BASIS FOR COST ESTIMATE	TOTAL
Equipment	for 15 preschoolers, shared with toddlers	$2,000
TOTAL CATEGORY V: EQUIPMENT		**$2,000**

CATEGORY VI: SPACE

ITEM	BASIS FOR COST ESTIMATE	TOTAL
Space	3,000 sq.ft. @$1/sq.ft./yr./8-month period	$2,000
Utilities and maintenance	Based on previous experience	2,533
TOTAL CATEGORY VI: SPACE		**$4,533**

Exhibit 3

MLKCCC — 8-Month Budget, Pineby Breakdown continued

CATEGORY VII: OTHER COSTS

ITEM	BASIS FOR COST ESTIMATE	TOTAL
Overhead	@ 10% of personnel	$7,475
Telephone	Installation & use	500
Printing		126
Insurance		266
Subscriptions, books, etc.		100
Miscellaneous, postage		925
TOTAL CATEGORY VII: OTHER COSTS		**$9,392**

CATEGORY VIII: DPW ADMINISTRATIVE COSTS

ITEM	BASIS FOR COST ESTIMATE	TOTAL
	1/19 of total program costs categories I - VII	
	1/19 of $103,212	
TOTAL CATEGORY VIII: DPW ADMINISTRATIVE COSTS		**$5,432**

GRAND TOTAL - LOCAL SHARE		**$ 27,161**
GRAND TOTAL - STATE SHARE		**$ 81,483**
GRAND TOTAL - PROJECT		**$ 108,644**

Exhibit 4

MLKCCC — Personnel Policies of the Hospital

SUMMARY

1. 10 sick days per year.

2. 10 vacation days per year.

3. Half the cost of tuition up to $400 per year for courses relating to work of the employee.

4. Child care employees work 7 1/2 hour day with a 1/2 hour break. Work in shifts between 7:00 a.m. and 5:30 p.m.

5. Compensatory time up to 8 hours can be accumulated for attending meetings that go past regular working day.

6. 3 personal leave days per year.

7. Following paid holidays: New Year's Day; Martin Luther King's Birthday; Memorial Day; July 4th; Labor Day; Thanksgiving Day; Christmas Day.

Exhibit 5

MLKCCC — A Teaching Note on Title XX and Other Government Sources of Funds

The Martin Luther King Center's story takes place in an era when the major source of funding for early care and education, other than Head Start, was Title XX of the Social Security Act. This teaching note is intended to give some information about Title XX, its place in funding chronology, its provisions, and its relation to funding policies of 1999.

The first major federal funding for child care was Title IV-A of the Social Security Amendments, passed in 1969. It was an opportunity for massive expansion for two reasons: (1) it was an open-ended funding stream, which means that the federal government would reimburse the states no matter how much they spent; (2) it had a 75% federal to 25% state funding formula. Local contributions, private contributions, and even United Way allocations to existing programs could be offered as the 25% match that would draw down a 75% federal share.

States could use local "donated funds," public or private, as the match. Some states required a local match as a way of attracting these federal dollars without cost to the state. Communities found that by donating existing resources, they could greatly multiply the total amount available for child care. The open-ended approach of the initial IV-A legislation was soon replaced by a fixed allocation.

Title XX, offering 100% federal funding, replaced Title IV-A as the major federal support for child care. A match was no longer federally required. Many states continued the match as a state requirement, or set up voluntary programs, where local communities that donated funds could get 75% federal money through the state, by contributing a match.

Title IV-A is long gone, replaced by Title XX, then by the Child Care and Development Block Grant, and then the Child Care Development Fund. After 1990, Title XX still exists, available to the states to use for child care and other purposes. Some policies and rules of Title XX are compared with those of newer legislation, below.

Services. When using Title XX to fund child care, some states funded only centers, while a few other states also paid for family child care homes in agency-based "systems."

Title XX was and is a block grant. That means the states receive the federal money in a block, or lump sum, and they can decide how to use it, within limits. Title XX had broad limits. It could be used for almost any social service: child care, elder services, services to the retarded, special needs or a wide range of other human services.

Exhibit 5

MLKCCC — A Teaching Note on Title XX and Other Government Sources of Funds continued

Eligibility of children for federal funding. With Title XX, states could use the money for eligible children, and they could define eligibility, within federal limits. To receive free child care, the children had to be from low-income families. States could choose to serve families earning moderate incomes (up to 115% of the median) if the parents paid a sliding fee based on income. Later, these federal restrictions were removed, leaving states completely free to define eligibility for fee-paying parents. Few states chose to serve the upper range permitted, although some set policies that would permit families who entered child care with low income to improve their income without losing their child care.

Currently the most-used funding streams for child care have substantially narrowed eligibility. None of them permits children to receive subsidy if their family is at or even near the median. The emphasis is now on poverty. CCDBG serves low-and moderately low-income families, without permitting them to increase their earnings. Welfare-related titles serve children of Welfare recipients, or, in a few states, children of families at the same income level as Welfare recipients.

Administration. Title XX was usually administered by state Welfare Departments or Social Service agencies. In most states, the Legislature appropriated state funds to pay for the services. The Title XX state agency then contracted for child care programs, paid them, and then claimed federal reimbursement under Title XX.

Funds to child care programs were spent in several ways. In some states, the state contracted with "umbrella agencies", one in each region. That umbrella agency (the Prime Contractor) then subcontracted with, funded, and monitored the child care centers. This system, begun with Title IV-A funds, was continued in some states with Title XX. The state's funding policies were interpreted to the centers by the umbrella agency. In those states, much of the paperwork was done by the umbrella administering agency.

Most states contracted directly with child care centers or agencies. Some of these states contracted for some of the "slots" in a program, while leaving other "slots" available to the general fee-paying public. (For "slots," see Appendix 1, Glossary.) This policy enabled them to avoid segregating eligible children in separate programs. Other states did not seek a socioeconomic mix, and contracted for the whole program.

The contracting child care agencies had to meet state rules and policies, and complete extensive paperwork. The payment was a reimbursement; i.e., the program first provided the service, and then could bill the state. There were no grants, and no up-front money under Title XX, or under CCDBG as currently administered by the states.

Exhibit 5

MLKCCC — A Teaching Note on Title XX and Other Government Sources of Funds continued

Vouchers. In a few states, some of the Title XX funds were used in a vendor/voucher funding mechanism designed for maximum parent choice. With a voucher, a parent could choose care for an individual child, and that program would be authorized to receive state subsidy after providing the service. The states that used this mechanism made the system as simple as possible for the parent and the child care program. A voucher agency absorbed the red tape and paperwork, and fronted the money in a complex administrative system.

In 1991, CCDBG required the states to enable parent choice, which stimulated all the states to develop vouchers. Vouchers are now far more common, and there are now a variety of voucher models, including paying the parents. There is less attention paid to monitoring quality than existed under the previous vendor/voucher systems.

Matching Dollars. There are no matching requirements for Title XX, or for the newer CCDBG. States receive 100% federal money. However, some states have continued to require the matching arrangements they had set up prior to the passage of Title XX.

Current Funding Streams: Child Care and Development Fund (CCDF)

The major federal direct funding stream for child care, along with Head Start and various education programs for young children with special needs, is the Child Care Development Fund. Merged in this newer funding are two separate streams: the Child Care and Development Block Grant, and several welfare-related federal-funding streams.

Welfare Funding Folded into CCDF. In 1995, the Congress merged some of the different welfare-related titles in a Child Care and Development Fund, combining CCDBG with the Welfare titles. However, the Welfare titles require federal matching, while CCDBG is 100% federal.

10. Good Shepherd Child Care Center

In December 1997 the Good Shepherd Child Care Center had been in operation for a year and a half. Located in the working class neighborhood of a medium-sized western city, it served 52 preschool children. Because of the high quality of its programs, and because there were no other comparable child development programs in the vicinity, Good Shepherd had never had any problem filling all its available places.

Katherine Shea was giving serious consideration to the possibility of expanding her program. She had learned in December that space immediately adjacent to hers would become available on July 1, 1998. Expansion would involve nothing more difficult than opening the doors between Good Shepherd's space and that of the building's next-door tenant, who would be leaving.

Because of the demand for enrollment in Good Shepherd, Ms. Shea expected no difficulty in registering 80 children, the total number the newly expanded space could accommodate. A seasonal reduction in enrollment was typical in the months of June, July and August, but starting in September 1998, she expected no problem in attracting families to enroll children.

In fact, the seasonal drop-off in attendance was the only thing that concerned Ms. Shea. During the summer of 1996 she had been unable to meet her payroll in August, when enrollments were down. The check from the state for subsidized tuition for 40 eligible children had not arrived on time. When there are changes in the numbers of children in a contract, payments from the state are likely to be delayed a month or even more. She was aware of the fact that there would probably be a cash flow problem every summer. She wondered to what extent a move to a larger program in July would magnify the cash flow problem.

She decided to do a cash flow projection for twelve months (January - December 1998) to see how serious the problem might be after the 80 children were enrolled.

Assignment: Do a 12-month cash flow projection for Ms. Shea, for the calendar year 1998. Use a computer spread sheet, or use ledger paper with 13 columns or more. Follow the format in your textbook for cash flow. The following materials will give you most of the information you need for estimating the monthly cash flow.

An important point to remember is that the money withheld from employees' paychecks in order to pay their taxes is not cash for the center. From the moment it is withheld, that money belongs to IRS and not to the center. Therefore, it is easiest to keep it out of the cash flow by leaving it in the employee's salary for the cash flow purposes. A director who spends this money during times it is not yet due at IRS is risking serious time in jail.

A copy of the Good Shepherd budget for 1997-1998 is included below as Exhibit 1. Ms. Shea had already done a budget projection based on 80 children for the first 6 months in expanded space: this budget is Exhibit 2. Exhibits 3, 4 and 5 are relevant information that Ms. Shea has pulled together to help her project her cash flow between January 1, 1998 and December 31, 1998.

Exhibit 1

Good Shepard Child Care Center
Operating Budget, July 1, 1997 - June 30, 1998

52 children full-day

EXPENDITURES

1 Director	$ 29,000
2 Teachers @ $17,000	34,000
8 Aides, part-time @ $10,000	40,000
1 Social worker, half-time @ $17,000	8,500
1 Bookkeeper, half-time @ $15,000	7,500
1 Nurse, 15% time @ $19,000	2,450
Personnel Sub-Total	**$121,450**
Fringes @ 15%	18,217
TOTAL PERSONNEL	**$139,667**
Food	$ 20,500
Supplies	4,800
Office equipment, replacement	3,200
Other equipment, replacement	3,500
Maintenance	8,500
Rent	16,000
Staff training	2,500
Transportation	2,400
TOTAL OTHER THAN PERSONNEL	**$ 61,400**
TOTAL EXPENSES	**$201,067**

INCOME

12 children: private tuitions and community scholarship fund @ $73/week x 50 weeks	$ 43,800
40 children: Title XX contract with Welfare Department @ $73/week	146,000
Food Program	9,000
Fundraising	1,200
TOTAL INCOME	**$200,000**

Exhibit 2

Good Shepard Child Care Center
Projected Operating Budget for 80 Children

July 1 - December 31, 1998

EXPENSES

1 Director	$ 14,500
4 Teachers @ $17,000/yr.	34,000
12 Aides, part-time @ $12,000/yr.	36,000
1 Social worker, half-time @ $17,000/yr.	4,250
1 Bookkeeper, half-time @ $15,000/yr.	3,750
1 Nurse, 25% time @ $19,000/yr.	2,375
Personnel Sub-Total	**$ 94,875**
Fringes @ 20%	18,975
TOTAL PERSONNEL	**$113,850**
Food	$ 15,250
Supplies	3,200
Office equipment, replacement	1,600
Other equipment, replacement.	1,750
Maintenance	4,750
Rent	12,500
Staff training	3,000
Transportation.	1,850
TOTAL OTHER THAN PERSONNEL	**$ 43,900**
TOTAL EXPENSES	**$157,750**

INCOME

30 children: private tuitions and community scholarship fund @ $73/week x 25 weeks	$ 54,750
50 children: contract with state @ $73/week	91,250
Food Program	9,000
Fundraising	3,000
TOTAL INCOME	**$158,000**

Exhibit 3

Good Shepard Child Care Center
Estimated State Payments, 1997 Calendar Year

MONTH	NUMBER OF CHILDREN	AMOUNT BILLED FOR THE MONTH	AMOUNT REC'D IN THAT MONTH
January	40	$12,556	$12,556 for December
February	40	12,556	12,556 for January
March	40	12,556	12,556 for February
April	40	12,556	12,556 for March
May	40	12,556	12,556 for April
June	40	12,556	12,556 for May
July	50	15,700	12,556 for June
August	50	15,700	0
September	50	15,700	31,400 for July/August
October	50	16,125	15,700 for September
November	50	16,125	16,125 for October
December	50	16,125	16,125 for November

Exhibit 4

Good Shepard Child Care Center
Estimated State Payments, 1997 Calendar Year

Salaries: Teachers and non-classroom staff got a large raise in 1997; a one-year salary freeze was discussed at that time with staff, since the center was so new, and is still acceptable as long as extra people are hired to deal with additional children. However, we have difficulty recruiting aides at $10,000. Raised aides to $12,000, and expected to hire some of them full-time, depending on recruitment. Budgeted equivalent of 6 full-time aides.

Bookkeeper is committed elsewhere for the other 50% of her time; has agreed to try to do the work for the center on the same half-time basis, even though the center is larger than it was.

Food and **Training** will vary by the number of children. I roughly divided current expenditures by 52 children; multiplied by 80.

Raised figures somewhat for **Maintenance, Supplies,** and **Staff Training,** because of additional children. I will be careful about spending on supplies and staff training until I have a better picture of enrollment.

Rent will be higher; we know the figure.

Income: Kept fees the same. If expenses are higher, we can raise both parents' and the state fee to $75 next year; welfare is willing to agree to $75. I plan to raise the fees in October if I clearly need the extra money.

This budget is based on an expectation that additional fee-paying parents will be attracted to the center and will bring a little more stability to the budget, since they will pay a little in advance, causing no cash flow problems. We expect the recruitment to succeed because of the reputation of the center. The ratio of state-funded to fee-paying children has been changed with more fee-paying parents.

However, the total income is going to be lower than projected because of lower enrollment during the summer months. See notes on the next page.

Exhibit 5

Good Shepard Child Care Center
Additional Notes Regarding Cash Flow

1. All employees are paid twice a month, on the 10th and the 25th.

2. Fringe benefits are paid quarterly (15th of March, June, September, and December).

3. Withholding taxes are paid quarterly to the IRS (on the same schedule as fringe benefits), and average 20% of payroll.

4. Food costs are paid as they are incurred.

5. Supplies are purchased in the following pattern: $1500 in January and in July, during sales; $300 every other month (Feb., April, June, Aug., Oct., Dec.). This pattern has proved effective, and should continue. Because of the additional children, I plan to spend $2000 in July, and in January; and to spend $400 every other month.

6. Office equipment and other equipment are budget estimates, and can be broken into 12 equal monthly payments to represent the approximate cash outflow.

7. Maintenance and rent are paid by the 10th of each month, for that month.

8. Staff training: if we expand our space and hire new staff, I would expect to use all this money in the beginning of July for staff development and consultation on environment design.

9. Transportation is paid on the 15th of each month, for that month's costs.

10. The state is paying $73 per week from now until July, when a new contract is signed. The state agency has indicated that we could negotiate a new rate, but not more than $75 per week, for up to 60 children. Paying parents cannot be charged less than the state pays; ideally, parents and the state would pay the same. I am not going to raise fees right away because we want to increase enrollment to 80 children as rapidly as we can, and the higher fees might prevent our growth. I plan to raise the fees, if I do, in October.

11. I would expect the pattern of enrollment over the summer to look approximately as follows, assuming we can open to our new capacity on July 1.

	JUNE	JULY	AUGUST	SEPTEMBER
Private tuition	12	10	10	30
State funds	40	50	50	50

Exhibit 5

Good Shepard Child Care Center
Additional Notes Regarding Cash Flow
continued

If the enrollment follows the trends we have found in the past, it might drop to 75 in mid-October, rise back to 80 by January 1, drop off to 75 in May, and dwindle to 65 over the summer.

12. Parents pay on the 1st and the 15th of each month, in advance for the following half-month period.

13. For state reimbursement, we submit an invoice on the last day of each month for the month that has just ended. We are paid about three-and-a-half weeks later. Except in rare instances of prolonged illness, children's attendance at the center has been excellent. The state reduces its payments if attendance is not at 80%, but that should not influence our cash flow projections. Contracts are renegotiated each July, and that slows down the payment process. Payment for July is not received until the end of September, and comes in along with the payment for the month of August. See Exhibit 3 for State Payment Schedule.

14. I'm trying to remember that our cash outlays for food and transportation will vary proportionally with the number of children actually served.

15. I anticipate beginning the one-year cash flow projection in the month of January with a cash balance of $3400.

11a. Wakefield Children's Center: Program Budget

The Wakefield Children's Center was serving preschool children in 1988. In 1989, they contracted with the state to care for abused children as well. In 1990, they developed a family child care satellite system. Caregivers were recruited to care for children in homes, with the central agency collecting the fees, and paying the caregiver an amount that covers all her expenses for the children, her salary, and the central costs of recruitment, supervision, training, and support.

As they entered the planning for 1992, they expected the state to purchase 60 full-time spaces in their preschool program. Of these, 10 would be cases of child abuse paid for at a special rate by the state, and the other 50 would be children of low-income or welfare parents. Another 60 children, none of them cases of child abuse, would be enrolled in the family child care homes. That was the pattern the state had purchased in 1991.

The total projected budget for 1992 follows (Exhibit 1). The first item is personnel costs. The family child care providers are not included in personnel costs because they are considered to be independent contractors. Wakefield will purchase family day care for 60 children at $16 a day from the family day care providers. The providers will use this amount to cover all their expenses as well as their compensation. Food, supplies, equipment, and earnings all come out of the $16 fee paid to the family child care providers.

The state department that purchases services has told them that their budget figures are not presented in adequate detail. To get state funding next year, they must:

1. Separate family day care costs from preschool costs;

2. Figure out how much more they are spending on abused children than on other preschool children, and;

3. Report their projected costs by functions: care and teaching, administration, occupancy, health, nutrition, transportation, social services, and training.

Exhibit 1
Project Budget 1992
Wakefield Children's Center

Personnel. $371,445

Rent 24,000

Utilities 10,500

Repair and maintenance. 7,000

Insurance. 14,000

Office supplies. 2,900

Educational supplies. 6,800

Kitchen supplies 1,000

Food 46,830

Other supplies 500

Accounting services 1,500

Audit 4,000

Communications. 5,700

Staff development. 2,800

Mileage reimbursement 4,900

Transportation. 29,500

Equipment replacement. 525

Other costs 4,180

Purchase of family child care 240,000

   GRAND TOTAL **$778,080**

Exhibit 2

Personnel Breakdown 1992
Wakefield Children's Center Budget

Director . . . .$ 26,000

Secretary. 17,680

Bookkeeper 50% 8,840

Family Day Care Coordinator 25,000

Family Day Care Monitor 23,920

Head Teacher. 22,960

Head Teacher 75%. 17,940

2 Teachers 41,600

Teacher 75% 14,820

2 Assistant Teachers 30,280

Teacher Aide 13,320

Teacher Aide 50% 6,588

Social Worker 18,720

Janitor/Driver 50% 9,260

Cook 16,640

2 Senior Aides. 21,216

Total Salaries **$314,784**

Fringes @ 18% 56,661

TOTAL PERSONNEL **$371,445**

Assignment: Read the section of the book on program budgeting. Answer the state's request for more detail on items (1) and (2). Prepare a program budget, separating costs in three columns: the preschool; the family child care; and the costs for abused children over and above the base preschool cost.

First, take the budget (Exhibit 1) and its line items, and spread these items across the different programs. You can do this assignment on a computer spreadsheet, or with a pencil and ledger paper. Either way, set up four columns of figures to the right of the line items. Label the heads of the columns as follows:

LINE-ITEMS	PRESCHOOL	ABUSED CHILDREN	FAMILY CHILD CARE	TOTAL

The first column is the separated-out cost of your preschool program. The second column is any *additional* expenditures you are making for the abused children, for whom you are paid a higher rate. The third column is your family child care program's costs. The last column is your totals. These totals add up to the total budget. With that known, figure out how to spread your costs across the different programs. Use the four worksheets in the book.

The budget by itself does not give you enough information to spread your personnel costs across the different programs. You need a breakdown of the personnel expenses. The breakdown is Exhibit 2.

11b. Wakefield Children's Center: Cost Analysis by Function

Assignment: Read the textbook on functional cost analysis. If you did assignment 11a, you have done a program budget. This assignment, (11b), calls for a functional cost analysis for one of your programs, the preschool program. You are responding to the third request made by the state for further cost detail on your programs.

Analyze your projected costs by functions: care and teaching; administration; occupancy; nutrition; transportation; health; social services; and training. Use the 4 worksheets on pages 84-90.

As you analyze your costs, be clear on the difference between program budgeting and functional cost analysis. They are two different tools. Functional cost analysis is a subset of program budgeting. Use your program budget for the preschool program for the numbers you need in the cost analysis.

This assignment does not ask you to analyze costs for all the programs, but only for the preschool program. Use the four worksheets printed in this book. You will set up columns for the eight functions, and spread the costs across the columns for each line item. You'll do separate worksheets for personnel and for supplies, and then you'll put all the costs together in the 8 columns.

The final step is to set up a budget where the names of the functions become the line items on the left-hand side of your paper, with the cost for each function showing as the expenses. You can add the broken-down line items as sub-heads under each function if you choose to look at a line-item budget organized by functions.

12. Marketing Jack and Jill

When Jack Sanchez married Jill Langton, it seemed like a marriage made in heaven. At that time, Jack wanted to leave his job in a large corporation in order to be in business for himself. He planned to start a children's program. Jill had just graduated from college with a specialization in early childhood education. As a teenager, she had lived for four years in Denmark, where she worked as an aide in a child care center.

Ten years ago, they started the Jack and Jill Child Care Center together. It was fully enrolled after the first year. The program served 100 3-to-5 year old children, and was open from 7 a.m. to 7 p.m. Jack found that the going rate at that time for child care in the community was $60 a week, so Jack and Jill charged $58.

The program is located in a converted small church. As its owners envision the facility, it could be quite attractive; but there has never been enough money to fix it up. The trash bins, for example, are on the front side of the building. There is clean linoleum on the floors but no carpeting. The outdoor and indoor equipment is about the same as that of other centers in the area.

Since the second year, the center operated with five groups of four-year-olds, twenty in each group. For the first six years, Jill taught in the center herself and trained the staff. Now she is home with two young children, but she continues to plan and participate in staff development.

Jill has seen a lot of high quality programs in Denmark, and she received a good professional education in this country. She knows that Jack and Jill is not as good as the centers she knew in Denmark and others she has seen in other states. But she feels that her program is the best in the geographic area where it is located. Of course she would never say this publicly because the other center directors and staff are her friends. She wouldn't want to brag.

After the first year, the center made 4.5% profit in each of the next five years. At that point, several new centers drained off some of the enrollment. There is no longer a waiting list. In order to keep their enrollment up, the center has reconfigured its classrooms. The center now includes two-year-olds with young threes in three of their groups (15 in each group), and operates two groups of old threes and young fours, and one group of old fours. Three of the six groups are under-enrolled.

Staffing costs are up, so the center must charge higher fees. The going rate in the community is now $90 per week, but two centers charge $95. The higher the fees, Jack believes, the fewer people will be able to enroll their children. But even $95 doesn't seem to be enough to cover the expenses of staffing now that the center has six groups. It feels as though the center may not make a profit this coming year.

Jack and Jill have decided to re-do their brochure to see if they can attract more parents. The brochure has a picture of the center on the front panel, and the message: "Put your child in this picture." The photograph shows the building, and it looks "about like any other good center" as Jack puts it. There are no people in the picture. Inside there is a drawing of Jack and Jill, the nursery rhyme characters, carrying a pail of water up a hill. The message says: "Check us out." These statements are made with boxes next to them, checklist style:

☐ Our fees are reasonable, $95 per child. Your second child will get a reduced rate.

☐ We are licensed by the state, and approved by local health and safety officials.

☐ Our location is convenient. (See the map on the back panel.)

☐ Our teachers are professionally trained to work with young children.

☐ We're open from 7 a.m. to 7 p.m.

☐ We offer nutritious meals.

This second panel makes its points briefly, with a lot of white space to set them off.

The third panel is much more densely typed. It summarizes center policies, with quite a lot of detail, including items such as these examples:

- A health assessment is required before enrolling your child. Immunizations must be up to date.

- The center requires that parents pick up their children on time. There is a late fee of $25 for every 15 minutes of parent tardiness.

- You should plan to attend our parent meetings once a month in the evening.

- Written permission from parents is required in order for your child to participate in field trips.

The back panel has the address and telephone number of the center, a small map and the message: "Call us for an appointment. Check us out!"

Last week, a corporation in the area offered financial help for Jack and Jill to become accredited. This offer came as a surprise to the owners. It was made to 5 centers in the area nominated by parent/employees at the corporation.

The company would pay all the accreditation fees, and would offer an incentive grant of $5000 for physical improvements. After the center becomes accredited, they would make a "reward" grant to enable the center to change its stationery and its brochure to let parents know that it is accredited. They require that the center be within the ratio/and group size range as defined in the accreditation standards.

As the director, Jack is not sure about this. He has never tried to put his center forward as better than other centers in the area. Further, he's fearful that accreditation would mean he might have to have smaller groups and lower ratios. He's already been stretched to make it, and is seriously considering raising fees to $99. If accreditation required him to have even more staff, the fees he might have to charge could become prohibitive, and parents would not enroll in his center.

- Exhibit 1 is Jack and Jill's current budget, amended.
- Exhibit 2 is the staffing patterns for accreditation.

As Jack and Jill talk over their options, they realize that they need to do something to bring in more dollars on the income side of their budget. They enjoyed the early years of owning their own center, but ten years have gone by and they seem to have reached, at best, a plateau in their careers. There is a need for change. Potential options are:

Option 1: Becoming accredited
Maybe if they were accredited, and also aggressively marketed to parents at the corporation and elsewhere, they could charge higher fees than other centers. It sounds frightening. There are no accredited centers in this area. Would accreditation add more expenditures? Could it generate more income if Jack and Jill are strategic in using it? Would the income it brings in be greater than the costs?

Option 2: Providing new child care services

Maybe they need to be more responsive to family needs in a changing economic environment. Some services they thought of were:

- Adding a satellite family child care network
- Adding a school-age program
- Offering part-time options
- Offering drop-in care
- Serving infants and toddlers

Are there others? How feasible would it be to add one or more? What would be the effect on the budget?

Option 3: Providing other services for parents

Maybe they should consider offering other services that parents could purchase on a fee-for-service basis. They've heard of centers that offer haircuts, take-out meals, stay-late services, and other services to parents. Should Jack and Jill try to find out how parents would feel about such services? Would parents be willing to pay for them?

Other information you need:

- All the income received by the program is based on fees.
- The fee charged is $4125 per child per year, paid by parents, government, or a combination.
- The center has another room that could be used for an additional group of children, although the new group would have to be smaller than the two groups currently fully enrolled.

Jack and Jill Assumptions about Staffing Patterns:

6 groups as follows:

Group 1.   Capacity 15 twos/young threes. Only 12 enrolled 9/25/95.

Group 2.   Capacity 15 twos/young threes. Only 12 enrolled.

Group 3.   Capacity 15 twos/young threes. Fully enrolled.
Current staffing in Groups 1, 2, and 3:
.75 lead teacher
1 teacher
1 assistant teacher

Group 4.   Capacity 20 threes. 17 enrolled.

Group 5. Capacity 20 threes/young fours. 15 enrolled.
Current staffing:
   1 lead teacher
   1 teacher
   .75 assistant teacher

Group 6. Capacity 22 fours. 12 fours enrolled.
Current staffing:
   .75 lead teacher
   .75 teacher
   1 assistant teacher

When a teacher is absent, the director or the secretary is qualified to substitute. Usually they have enough staff so that they seldom hire substitutes.

Assignment: Prepare a personnel budget for the center at current enrollment, and at capacity enrollment. What are Jack and Jill's current operating ratios and group size, and how do they compare with the accreditation criteria?

Think specifically about the income side of the budget. What are the ways that Jack and Jill can add more revenues to offset expenditures? Flesh out Jack and Jill's thinking about their options; add your ideas. Identify the pros and cons of the different options.

Questions:
Prepare notes to discuss with the group:

- What do you think of Jack and Jill's marketing strategy up to now?
- Are there improvements you would make in their brochure? Make concrete suggestions.
- Should Jack and Jill change their name? Why or why not?
- Should Jack and Jill change the way they think about their fees? Why or why not?
- Should Jack and Jill change the way they provide their service? Why or why not?
- Are there potential parents not currently using center care whom Jack and Jill could attract with a different marketing perspective? How could they find out?
- What would be the effect of accreditation on fees and on the market? How could they find out?
- What's their best option?
- What would you do if you were Jack and Jill?

Exhibit 1

The Jack and Jill Child Care Center
1995-1996 Amended Budget

Based on 93 children expected (Current enrollment 83 children, 9/25/95)

EXPENSES

Owner/Management draw . . . .$ 38,000

Administrative services
(payroll, legal, accounting @ $1000/mo) 12,000

Garbage disposal/snow removal ($150/mo) 1,800

Repairs ($400/mo) 4,800

Marketing ($50/mo) 600

Postage 2,000

Telephone ($200/mo) 2,400

Office supplies 4,000

Classroom supplies (93 children @ $100/child/yr) 9,300

Kitchen supplies (93 children @ $50/child/yr, not including infants) 4,900

Food ($750/child/yr) 69,750

Professional dues 500

Licensing fee 200

Equipment replacement/reserve ($1000/yr) 1,000

Mortgage 15,000

Cleaning and maintenance service ($200/wk) 10,400

Taxes 7,000

Utilities ($2/sq ft) 20,000

TOTAL **$203,650**

Depreciation not included

Personnel

Assistant director @ $25,415 + 20% benefits $30,500

Cook, 4 hrs/day @ $5.50/hour 5,500

1 Floater @ $12,480 + 20% benefits 14,976

Substitutes 10,000

Staff for Groups 1 and 2* 65,000

Staff for Group 3* 32,500

Staff for Group 4* 48,000

Staff for Group 5* 48,000

Staff for Group 6* 42,300

Consultants: Staff Development (Jill) 5,000

TOTAL PERSONNEL **$301,776**

TOTAL EXPENDITURES **$505,426**

Exhibit 1

The Jack and Jill Child Care Center
1995-1996 Amended Budget continued

Based on 93 children expected (Current enrollment 83 children, 9/25/95)

INCOME

Parent fees 93 children @ $95 x 50 weeks x 95% utilization $419,663

If enrolled at 107 children @ $95 x 50 weeks x 95% $482,838

If enrolled at 107 children @ $100 x 50 weeks x 95% utilization $508,250

Average Salary Assumptions, Classroom Staff

Lead Teacher @ $16,000/year + 20% benefits. $19,200

Teacher @ $15,000/year + 20% benefits $18,000

Assistant @ $12,000/year + 20% benefits $14,400

See Jack and Jill Assumptions about Staffing Patterns, in narrative.

Exhibit 2

Staffing Ratios in NAEYC Criteria for Accreditation 1998

AGE OF CHILDREN	GROUP SIZE*										
	6	8	10	12	14	16	18	20	22	24	30
Infants (birth–12 months)	1:3	1:4									
Toddlers (12–24 months)	1:3	1:4	1:5	1:4							
2-year-olds (24–30 months)		1:4	1:5	1:6							
2.5-year-olds (30–36 months)			1:5	1:6	1:7						
3-year-olds					1:7	1:8	1:9	1:10			
4-year-olds						1:8	1:9	1:10			
5-year-olds						1:8	1:9	1:10			
Kindergartners								1:10	1:11	1:12	
6- to 8-year olds								1:10	1:11	1:12	1:15
9- to 12-year olds										1:12	1:15

*Smaller group sizes and lower staff-child ratios have been found to be strong predictors of compliance with indicators of quality such as positive interactions among staff and children and developmentally appropriate curriculum. Variations in group sizes and ratios are acceptable in cases where the program demonstrates a very high level of compliance with criteria for interactions, curriculum, staff qualification, health and safety, and physical environment.

13a. Breaking Even at The Children's Place

Some of the parents at The Children's Place are complaining that the fees are too high. They want the Director to explain to them why they cannot reduce the fees to $3600 and take more children. You, as the Director, have decided to hold a meeting. You want to explain your fee policies in a way the parents can understand.

Assignment: Read the textbook section on break-even analysis.

(1) Prepare a break-even chart, showing at what number of children the center will break even at the current fee. Use 9 children for your "clump" of semi-variable costs. (There will be 4 "clumps" in a center of 36, and the cost of one clump is 1/4 of the total semi-variable costs.)

(2) Prepare a break-even chart to show parents the effect of the lower fee on the break-even point. Note you can make two charts, or you can show two different income lines on the same chart, possibly using two colors.

Exhibit 1

The Children's Place
Current Budget

EXPENSES

Advertising	$ 500
Classroom consumables	1080
Health consumables	120
Classroom equipment	500
Office equipment	360
Outdoor equipment	360
Food purchases	8,220
Kitchen supplies	600
Kitchen equipment	175
Substitutes	2,500
Insurance	900
Staff training	200
Janitorial services	1,560
Rent and improvements	7,120
License and building inspection	120
Office supplies and expenses	490
Postage	400
Printing	360
Telephone	750
Transportation	
Driver and vehicle	8,500
Field trips	240
Auto insurance	240
Audit	200
Miscellaneous	1,000
Work/Study students	3,500
Salaries	103,500
Benefits @ 15%	15,525
TOTAL EXPENDITURES	**$159,020**

INCOME

Fees $4125 for 36 children, parents, SPED, and state	$148,500
Bureau of Nutrition	8,000
Kappa Fund	4,400
TOTAL INCOME	**$160,900**

13b. Adding a Classroom at The Children's Place

The Children's Place has been operating for a number of years with four groups. Lately there has been a slight falling off in enrollment of four-year olds. The Board believes that if The Center adds an infant/toddler program, they will grow their own four-year-olds, and also enhance the reputation of the center as an important community service. There is a space that could be used for a small group, and they would even consider moving to another available space to provide two new rooms, one infants and one toddlers, if you recommend it. They ask that you, as the director, prepare useful information for them so they can decide.

First, they want to know the fixed costs of the center at present. To what extent does each of the separate rooms bring in enough revenue to cover the direct cost of what it does, plus its share of the fixed costs?

If we add another classroom of infants and toddlers, would that classroom be able to bring in enough revenue to cover the cost of the direct service, AND 1/5 of the fixed costs?

You are going to provide them with information using a simple break-even chart for each room, and one for the new program. First, you need to redo your budget with the new costs and the new income for the new program. Then you need to analyze the costs into fixed and variable. Use the simple form of break-even, with these steps for each classroom.

1. Plot the classroom's share of fixed costs on the bottom of the graph.

2. Plot a line for the variable costs (including the semi-variable costs in with the variable ones).

3. Plot an income line and then find the break-even point.

4. Analyze and discuss whether each classroom is breaking even.

5. Label all these charts "Current break-even data" and identify which classroom it is.

Making a graph of this type can be done in less than a minute. Do this for each classroom and then do it for the new, proposed infant/toddler group. You might try one chart in which the infant/toddlers' parents pay at the same rate as the threes and fours. Then you might do another one where they pay very high fees. You might try one in-between, for purposes of discussion.

For this use of break-even, you not only have to set fees, you also have to figure out the total fixed costs of the center, and how to allocate responsibility for those costs among the classrooms. If you add a fifth group, the other four groups will have a lower share of the fixed costs, so that the break-even graphs for those other classrooms will change. You might label the new graphs "Break-even data for _____ room if new infant/toddler group is added."

These charts are easy to make, so you can try out a lot of different things to present to your board. Use break-even graphs to prepare answers to the questions you think they might ask you, such as:

- Would the new classroom bring in enough money to cover its own operating costs (staff, space, equipment etc.)?

- Would it bring in enough to cover the fixed costs it adds to the center?

- Is any other classroom covering more than its own share of the fixed costs? Could its revenues be used to enable the center to open an infant/toddler classroom?

The budget you will use is a part of case #13a.

Glossary

Terms Used in Banking and Financial Management

"Acid test" ratio The "acid test" ratio is one of the common barometers used by banks in extending credit because it indicates the ability of an organization to meet its obligations. Cash plus any other assets that can be converted to cash *immediately* should equal or be greater than current liabilities. The formula used is the following:

$$\frac{\text{cash + receivables (net) + marketable assets}}{\text{current liabilities}}$$

Accounts receivable, or "receivables" All the items in which some other person or organization owes money to you that has not yet been paid. "Aging receivables" describes a scheduling of accounts receivable according to the length of time they have been outstanding. It shows which accounts are not being paid in a timely manner, and may reveal problems with accounts not easily collected.

Amortization The process of gradually paying off a liability on the installment plan over a period of time.

Assets The valuable resources, tangible property and property rights owned by an individual or an organization.

Attendance The number of children who actually came to the children's program on a particular day, or during a particular week, month or year.

Bad debts Accounts receivable that will never be collected.

Balance sheet An itemized statement that lists an organization's total assets and total liabilities, portraying its net worth at a given moment in time.

Bonding A form of insurance guaranteeing the customers of the children's program against loss through theft and/or damage by an employee of the organization.

Break-even analysis A method used to determine or portray the point at which an organization will neither make a profit nor incur a loss. At this point, the total dollars coming in will exactly offset the cost of providing the service to the number of children using it.

Budget A financial plan for a given period of time itemizing all the money that will be spent and itemizing, by sources of revenues, all the money that is expected to be received.

Budget justification or **budget rationale** A detailed narrative that explains why each item in the budget is determined at a particular amount.

Capital Any form of material wealth used or available for use in the production of more wealth.

Capital equipment Equipment, costing you more than $250, that you will use over a period of a number of years, rather than use up in one year.

Cash flow The actual movement of cash to operate the children's program: cash inflow compared with cash outflow. Used to offer a better indication of the organization's ability to meet its own obligations than the conventional net worth figure shown on an income and expense statement.

Cash flow cushion An amount of money kept in the program's bank account that is large enough to cover any temporary, expected, negative cash flow.

Cash position See *liquidity.*

Collateral Property, stocks, bonds, savings accounts, certificates of deposit, life insurance, and current assets, any or all of which may be held or offered to insure repayment of a loan.

Contract A legally binding agreement, whether written or oral, entered into by two parties. To be legally enforceable, a contract must have three elements: an offer, an acceptance of the offer, and an agreed upon "consideration." The consideration can be money that the person agrees to pay for the thing offered, or it can be anything else of value, such as a free space for a child in a program as payment for cleaning services.

Cooperative A form of organization, either for-profit or not-for-profit, that shares its assets with contributing members.

Corporation An artificial "person," or legal entity, created under government laws and given certain powers and responsibilities; a group of individuals or legal entities that voluntarily join together under the law to form a for-profit or a not-for-profit enterprise.

Costs All resources expended to produce the service in the children's program, including money, the value of things, and the value of time spent by individuals. Note that cost is not the same as price. Costs include the following:

> **Cash costs** All the out-of-pocket expenses in money, whether paid by check or cash.

> **Fixed costs** The costs that remain the same regardless of the number of children participating in the program.

> **In-kind costs** All the donated time of individuals who volunteer or work without receiving pay; donated equipment and supplies.

> **True costs** All the costs, both in-kind and cash.

> **Variable costs** The costs that vary with the number of children in the program, and differ with different numbers of children.

Current assets Cash and other items that will normally be turned into cash within one year, and assets that will be used up in the normal operations of the program within one year, but are presently on hand.

Current liabilities Amounts owed that will ordinarily be paid within one year. Such items include all accounts payable, wages payable, taxes payable, the current portion of a long-term debt, and interest payments.

Current ratio A ratio of a firm's current assets to its current liabilities.

Depreciation A reduction in the value of an asset over time. The most important causes of depreciation are wear and tear, and gradual obsolescence. For-profit organizations use a bookkeeping charge for depreciation to write off the original cost of the asset, minus expected salvage value, by equitably distributing charges against operations over its entire useful life. Guidance material from the Internal Revenue Service standardizes this practice. Small not-for-profit organizations, which have no tax advantage from depreciation, usually simplify their bookkeeping by replacing assets on a rotating schedule and ignoring depreciation charges.

Deviation The difference between planned expenditures (or income) and actual expenditures (or income), expressed either in amounts (dollars) or percentages.

Enrollment The number of children whose parents or guardians have agreed to send them to the children's program for a given period of time.

Entrepreneur An innovator with vision who recognizes opportunities, mobilizes the necessary resources, engages in the necessary planning, and organizes resources to bring a new service, product, or enterprise into reality.

Equity The monetary value of a property or an enterprise that is greater than the claims against it held by others.

Fees The price decided upon for the service, to be paid by parents/guardians, government, or a combination of payers, for each child.

Fringe benefits All money, in-kind insurance, vacations, and other benefits offered to a staff person over and above his or her wages. Fringe benefits include: employer share of FICA, Worker's Compensation, health and retirement plans, paid training, paid recreational programs, and counseling services.

FTE, or full-time equivalent The number of full-time children or staff that would result if part-time children or staff were added together. Example: 3 children enrolled Monday, Wednesday, and Friday, plus 3 children enrolled Tuesday and Thursday, represent 3 FTE children.

Functional cost analysis The use of uniform cost categories representing different functions of a children's program in order to compare costs from one program to another. Standard functions have been identified: care and teaching, social services, food services, health services, parent services and special events, administration, occupancy, and transportation.

Gross income All the money taken in by a program, prior to subtracting expenses. Gross income minus all expenses is **net income**.

Illiquid See *liquidity.*

Income and expense statement, also called a **profit and loss statement,** or an **income statement.** An itemized list of all income and all expenses for a given period of time. Income statements cast into the future are called *income projections.* They serve as tools for forecasting and estimating expected income and anticipated future expenditures.

In-kind See *costs.*

Interest A charge for a financial loan, usually a percentage of the amount loaned.

Liquidity   A term used to describe solvency, particularly of a for-profit business. It has special reference to the degree to which assets can be readily converted into cash without a loss. Also called **cash position.** If an organization's current assets cannot be converted into cash to meet its liabilities, it is said to be **illiquid.**

Long-term liabilities   Expenses that are incurred, but will not mature, or come due, in the short run.

Market   The number of people within the geographic area you serve and their spending of money, actual or potential, for the service you provide. Families who do not want or need a children's program are not in the market.

Market share   The percent of the market that you, as compared with other, similar children's programs, serve.

Net income   See *gross income.*

Net worth   The owner's equity in a proprietary business, represented by the excess of total assets over amounts owed (liabilities) at a given moment. Also, the net worth of an individual or a corporation as determined by deducting the amount of personal or corporate liabilities from the total value of personal or corporate assets.

Non-profit, or **not-for-profit**   See *profit.*

Occupancy costs   All expenditures for rent or mortgage payments, utilities, maintenance, and other costs associated with the physical facility.

Operating costs   The costs of running a program during a budget year, after the start-up period. See *start-up costs.*

OTP (other than personnel)   The part of the expense budget that covers all line items except personnel.

Partnership   A legal relationship created voluntarily by two or more persons who associate together as co-owners of a business for profit.

Payables or **accounts payable**   All the money (due to be paid) that you owe someone else at a given time.

Price   The amount a children's program charges for each participating child.

Principal   The main body of a financial holding, as distinguished from interest or revenues.

Profit The excess of revenues collected after all costs and expenses incurred are paid. A *for-profit* organization is a proprietorship, partnership, corporation, or cooperative that anticipates such excess will exist, although in reality it may not. A *not-for-profit* corporation is a legal entity created in anticipation that it will break even, serve the community, and use any excess revenues within the program. A for-profit organization may use profit to distribute to investors, and a not-for-profit organization may not.

Profit and loss statement See *income and expense statement.*

Pro forma A projection or estimate of what may result in the future from actions in the present. A pro forma financial statement is one that projects how the operations of the business will turn out if current assumptions prove correct.

Program budget A way of presenting financial information that identifies the costs of each program rather than lumping all costs together in a budget for the organization, when a single agency or organization runs more than one program. Program budgets make it possible to compare the costs of different programs.

Proprietorship or **sole proprietorship** A type of business organization in which one individual owns the business. Legally, the owner is the business, and personal assets are exposed to any liabilities of the business.

Receivables See *accounts receivable.*

"Slot" A space in a child care program for one child year. The term does not refer to a child, but to a unit of service, similar to the use of the word "bed" in hospital planning. Over the course of a budget year, a single "slot" may be occupied by several different children in succession. Similarly, a "slot" could be filled by several part-time children, who add up to one full-time child. See *FTE.*

Start-up costs One-time-only costs incurred in the period before a children's program is operating at its full budgeted capacity. Start-up costs include all the costs incurred before any children are enrolled, and also the costs of operating below an efficient level before the full number of children has been recruited and enrolled and has paid fees. **Operating costs,** in contrast, are the costs of running a program after the start-up period is over, the break-even point reached, and the program is operating efficiently in an annual budget cycle.

Sliding fee   A schedule of fees based on ability to pay.

Target market   The specific families, characterized by socioeconomic, demographic, physical/medical, and/or interest characteristics, which are identified as potential users of a children's program.

Tax credit   An amount that is subtracted, not from taxable income, but from the amount of tax owed, or the tax bill. Parents get a credit of 20% to 30% on their personal income tax for child care expenses. Working families get an additional Earned Income Credit, which is greatest for low-earning families.

Tax deduction   An expenditure that is a legitimate cost of doing business and is allowed by the IRS to be deducted from taxable income (as in the case of charitable gifts up to a cap). Total tax deductions will be subtracted from the amount earned in figuring taxes owed on profit.

Tort   Any wrongful act, damage, or injury done willfully, negligently, or in circumstances involving strict liability, but not involving breach of contract, for which a civil suit can be brought.

Utilization   A factor based on the past relationship between enrollment expectation and actual enrollment, that allows for the fact that there are lags between one child leaving a children's program, and its slot being filled by another child.

Voucher, vendor-voucher, certificate   A document or card that serves as proof of a third-party payment being made by a governmental agency for a particular child, as a result of a legal agreement.

Working capital   An excess of current assets over current liabilities that permits money to be available for carrying on the operations and cushioning cash flow problems.

Appendix 2
Useful Resources

American Institute of Certified Public Accountants, 919 Third Avenue, New York NY 10022, tel. (212) 581-8840. Contact: Manager, Accounting Aid Program. This organization may be able to locate free accountant assistance for needy programs.

Child Care Information Exchange is a magazine for directors of children's programs, published by Roger and Bonnie Neugebauer, C-44, PO Box 3249, Redmond, WA 98073-3249.

Child Care Resource and Referral Agencies (CCRR). There is now a national network of CCRR organizations across the country. They are an excellent source of help to children's programs; a source of data on needs in the area; and an important link between children's programs and employer funding streams. These agencies also assist parents in their search for services for their children. To find one in your area, call the National Association of Child Care Resource and Referral Agencies (NACCRRA), 1319 F Street NW, Suite 606, Washington, DC 20004-1106, tel. (202)-393-5501.

Grantsmanship Center, 1015 West Olympic Boulevard, Los Angeles, CA 90015. Large number of useful reprints on fundraising and financial management for non-profit, most of which is equally applicable to for-profits. Ask for list of reprints, especially *Program Planning and Proposal Writing, Guide to Accounting for Nonprofits,* and *Guide to Public Relations.*

The *Internal Revenue Service* offers valuable publications, such as Number 534, *Depreciation.* Many libraries have reference sets of IRS publications, which are also available at your local IRS office. You will find the IRS listed in the telephone book under U.S. Internal Revenue Service.

The Midwest Center for Nonprofit Leadership is located in the University of Missouri at Kansas City, The Henry W. Bloch School of Business and Public Administration, 5100 Rockhill Road, Kansas City MO 64110-2499, tel. 816-235-1169. The Center sponsors conferences and publications. Marie McArther is Director of the Early Childhood Division.

National-Louis College has established a center offering management training for directors, technology for directors, research, and publications. Paula Jorde Bloom, Director, Center for Early Childhood Leadership, National Louis University, 336 Crescent Drive, Lake Bluff, IL 60044-2706.

Small Business Administration is a federal agency with offices throughout the United States that offers publications, training sessions, and loans for small for-profit businesses. They also offer a program in which retired business people serve as consultants to small for-profit businesses. SBA is listed in the local telephone directory.

Wheelock College offers intensive summer courses for directors of children's programs on its campus in Boston, and year-round field courses in other cities. The same center is working with groups in various locations to establish a director credential. Wheelock's graduate school offers a number of master's programs, one of them in Leadership. The Taking the Lead Project, headed by Cecilia Alvarado, is working on director-credentialing in 4 locations. For more information on any of these initiatives, contact Taking the Lead, a national center for information on director credentialing. Ask for their publications lists, and in particular for the *Director Credential Matrix.* Contact: Bess Emanuel, Wheelock College Center for Career Development in Early Care and Education, 200 The Riverway, Boston MA 02215, tel. 617-734-5200 x2211.

Appendix 3
Useful Resources: Books

Child Care Center Resource and Business Kit; How to Open a Child Care Center. 1997. Available free from Kaplan Companies, Inc., P.O. Box 609, Lewisville, NC 27023-0609, 1-800-334-2014. www.Kaplanco.com.

Collins, J. and J. Porras. 1997. *Built to Last: Successful Habits of Visionary Companies.* NY: HarperBusiness.

Gross, M. and R. Bruttomesso (Eds.) 1995. *Financial and Accounting Guide.* NY: John Wiley & Sons.

Morgan, G. 1998. *A Hitchhiker's Guide to the Child Care Universe.* Washington, D.C. NACCRRA Course on the Internet, also print copy.

Neugebauer, R, and B. 1998. *The Art of Leadership: Managing Early Childhood Organizations.* Redmond, WA: Child Care Information Exchange. 2 Vols.

O'Connell, B. 1993. *The Board Members' Book.* NY: The Foundation Center.

Steckel, R. 1985. *Filthy Rich & Other Nonprofit Fantasies: Changing the Way Nonprofits Do Business in the 90's.* Berkeley, CA: Ten Speed Press.

Tracy, J. 1996. *Budgeting A La Carte: Essential Tools for Harried Business Managers.* NY: John Wiley & Sons.

Willer, B. (Ed) 1990. *Reaching the Full Cost of Quality.* Washington, DC: NAEYC.

Appendix 4

Time Line for Major Tasks for Center Start-up

Adapted from the Day Care Council of America, Inc., 1981

This time line is designed primarily for small single centers. The above assumes that you could take about a year to get started, particularly in large areas with complex regulatory systems. By concentrated planning and using the shortest length of time for each step, it could be done in half this projected time in many, but not all geographic areas.

ACTION STEP	1ST MONTH	2ND MONTH	3RD MONTH	4TH MONTH	5TH MONTH	6TH MONTH	7TH MONTH	8TH MONTH	9TH MONTH	10TH MONTH	11TH MONTH	12TH MONTH
1. Get licensing rules, zoning ordinances; ask about sanitation codes, fire & safety codes.	21 days											
2. Determine the demand for center care in community; decide what kind of center you will run.	45 days →											
3. Decide on the form or organization: partnership, corporation or proprietorship, and whether for-profit or not.	10 days											
4. File and receive corporation papers if a corporation; file a true name certificate if a proprietorship.		120 days			→							
5. File tax exemption forms if not-for-profit; federal and state.			60 –100 days			→				30 –180 days →		
6. Develop figures for an operating budget and a start-up budget.	45 days — revise as you get new information											

7. Decide on location and determine costs for building, purchasing, leasing or using donated space. Seek zoning variance if necessary. — 30–180 days

8. Plan for and obtain funding:
- Foundations — 30–352 days
- Grants — 30–260 days
- Bank loans — 30–90 days
- Contributions — ongoing
- Fundraisers — ongoing
- Self — ongoing

9. Get building ready for occupancy (including renovations if necessary).
Rental improvements
- by you or landlord — 30–90 days
- Purchase building — 30–260 days
- Donated space — 30–90 days
- New construction — 1–2 years

10. Apply for and receive approvals from health, building & fire safety. Apply for and receive license. — 30–60 days / 30–45 days

11. Order & purchase toys, furniture, food, equipment. — 30–90 days

12. Open utilities accounts (allow time for service to begin). — 30 days

13. Determine how many staff; write descriptions; recruit & hire staff. — 14–45 days

14. Train staff team; plan schedule & curriculum. — 20 days

15. Advertise, recruit & enroll children. — 30–60 days

Appendix 5

Sample (Prototype) Budgets

Full-Year Prototype Budget in a Low-Cost Region
Economy Model   July 1, 1998 - June 30, 1999

INCOME

Parent fees $100,000 x 95% utilization $95,000

Other sources might include: corporate subsidy; management
fee; fundraising; investment income; loan; voucher; special fees;
government contract; government registration fees; USDA;
transportation fees; drop-in care; special needs subsidy 428,070

TOTAL INCOME   **$523,070**

EXPENSES [based on 98 children (See *assumptions,* on pages 224–226)]

Personnel

Director 23,000

Other Administrators 10,000

Teachers 200,000

Cook (4 hrs/day @ $7/hr) 7,000

Substitutes 15,000

Sub-Total Personnel $255,000

Benefits @ 18% of Personnel Salaries 45,900

TOTAL PERSONNEL   **$300,900**

OTP EXPENSES (other than personnel)

Space rental (if donated space not available) 120,000

Utilities (@ $2 per sq. ft.) 17,500

Maintenance 9,000

Garbage disposal & snow removal (@ $100/month) 1,200

Marketing 500

Postage 1,200

Office supplies 2,500

Classroom supplies 20,000

Kitchen supplies 1,500

Food 45,570

Professional dues 500

Staff development 1,000

Licensing fee 200

Equipment replacement/reserve 1,000

Taxes (if for-profit) 500

TOTAL OTP EXPENSES   **$222,170**

TOTAL EXPENSES   **$523,070**

Full-Year Prototype Budget in a High-Cost Region
High-Quality Model   July 1, 1998 - June 30, 1999

INCOME

Parent fees $326,560 x 95% utilization $310,232

Unrelated business income; Corporate contract for priority enrollment;
   Government contract and vouchers; fundraising; investment income;
   loan; registration fees; transportation fees; USDA; other subsidy . . 735,809

TOTAL INCOME	**$1,046,041**

EXPENSES [based on 95 children (See *assumptions* on pages 224–226)]

Personnel

Director	37,000
Other administrative staff	33,000
Teachers	400,428
Support (Cook, Nurse)	30,000
Floater	12,500
Substitutes	25,000

Sub-Total Personnel . . . .$ 537,928

Benefits @ 30% of Personnel Salaries 161,378

TOTAL PERSONNEL	**$ 699,306**

OTP EXPENSES (other than personnel)

Space, if rental	180,000
Utilities (@ $2 sq. ft.)	25,000
Administrative & legal contract services (@ $2000/month)	24,000
Garbage disposal, snow removal, ice removal (@ $150/month)	1,800
Repairs ($800/month)	9,600
Marketing	5,000
Postage	5,000
Telephone ($200/month)	2,400
Office supplies	5,000
Kitchen supplies	4,900
Food ($780/child/year, not including infants/toddlers)	56,160
Professional dues	500
Staff development ($500/child/year)	10,875
Enrichment ($50/child/year)	4,750
Licensing fee	200
Equipment replacement/reserve (depreciation not included)	5,000
Transportation ($50/child/year)	4,750
Taxes (if for-profit)	1,500

TOTAL OTP EXPENSES	**$ 346,435**
TOTAL EXPENSES	**$1,045,741**

Assumptions about Personnel Expenses

1. **Benefits:** The center in the low-cost region is paying 18% benefits. The center in the high-cost region pays 30% benefits on higher salaries, due to a severe labor shortage and the greater need to attract and retain staff.

2. **Administration:** The director of the center in the low-cost region is paid $23,000/year and has a part-time bookkeeper and a part-time assistant. The director of the center in the high-cost region is paid $37,000/year and has a full-time assistant director (who is paid $25,000/year + 30% in benefits) and a half-time assistant.

3. **Cook:** The cook for the center in the low-cost region is employed 4 hours a day @ $7/hour. The high quality center in the high-cost area has budgeted for other support staff (such as a nurse), in addition to the cook, and is paying 30% in benefits. With its more generous line item for support staff, this center has the flexibility to offer the cook more working hours, and/or to pay a higher salary.

4. **Janitor or maintenance contract:** The center in a low-cost area pays $9/hour, but a labor shortage might make it hard to find and maintain staff at this estimate. The high quality-oriented center located in the higher cost area includes in its budget several items to cover maintenance. It allocates sufficient funds to cover the necessary expenses, including the $1800 annual contract for snow, ice and garbage removal, plus repairs at $800 per month.

5. **Teaching staff** (See Assumptions about Staffing a Group): In addition to what is listed, the center in the high-cost area is hiring a floater. Salaries in the two centers differ by 10 - 35%, as shown below.

AVERAGE SALARIES

Classroom Role	Lower-Cost Center	Higher-Cost Center
Teacher	$12,500	$15,600
Lead Teacher	$14,000	$18,720
Assistant Teacher	$10,200	$12,400
Kindergarten Teacher	$17,000	$19,000

6. **Substitutes:** In the high-cost area, the substitutes are budgeted at $40 a day for an expected fifteen days. In the low-cost areas, substitutes are budgeted at a lower cost, with a lower number of days expected.

Assumptions about Staffing a Group

Stagger staff hours to cover the long day. A very crude rule of thumb for the number of staff to employ *is roughly 2.75 FTEs per group.* This formula, however, is only for very crude estimating. You will also need to know how many children constitute a group.

Group Sizes:
The following numbers of children, by ages, define a group, for purposes of these two prototype budgets:

8 infants/toddlers	10 one-year olds
12 two-year olds	16 three-year olds
18 four-year olds	20 kindergarten children

Infant groups become toddler groups by adding 2 new children to the same group with same teacher.

One-year-old groups become two-year-old groups by adding 2 new children to same group with same teacher.

Assumptions about Parent Fees
High-Cost Area, Quality Center
95 Children, 1999

16 infants (2 groups) @ $75/week, totals $1,200/week $62,400/year

10 one-year-olds @ $70/week, totals $700/week $36,400/year

12 two-year-olds @ $65/week, totals $780/week $40,560/year

20 three-year-olds @ $60/week, totals $1,200/week $62,400/year

20 four-year-olds @ $60/week, totals $1,200/week $62,400/year

20 kindergartners @ $60/week, totals $1,200/week $62,400/year

General Assumptions

- There is not such a thing as "a" children's program cost. Budgets vary by the part of the country, by their own goals of quality, by what parents are able to pay, by their staff's willingness to stay, and by access to free space. They vary in their ability to pay good salaries and retain their staff.

- Budgets vary greatly by part of the country. The per-child cost in one area, like Boston, is double the per-child cost in another, like Atlanta.

- A high level of funding does not assure quality. Well-funded programs can be low in quality. But few programs achieve quality without a basic level of resources.

- As you consider your own circumstances, use these two prototype budgets only as a point of departure. The center in a low-cost area is not offering rock-bottom quality, because this center wants to achieve quality as much as it can. It seeks additional sources of support, but it lacks the resources to achieve its goals fully. The center in a high-cost area is also in a high resource area. It can charge parents more, and has access to other sources of support.